Camo Mania
New Disruptive Patterns In Design

CA
MO

Camo Mania
New Disruptive Patterns In Design

First published and distributed by
viction:workshop ltd.

viction:ary™

viction:workshop ltd.
Unit C, 7·F, Seabright Plaza, 9-23 Shell Street,
North Point, Hong Kong
Url: www.victionary.com   Email: we@victionary.com
☐ @victionworkshop
🐦 @victionary_
📷 @victionworkshop

Edited and produced by viction:ary

Concepts & art direction by Victor Cheung
Book design by viction:workshop ltd.
Text by Alisha Tang

ISBN 978-988-77746-4-8
Printed and bound in China

I first became interested in camouflage not because of its inherent military link but for its playfulness — a subtle game of hide and reveal that takes so many forms. I find it fascinating whilst studying and still to this day that so many kinds of camouflage have been developed by nations around the globe for diverse terrains. One can become bogged down with their various iterations and subtle evolutions but I prefer to celebrate their breadth and immerse myself in their patterns. Over the years I've tried hard not to hoard too many original garments but the truth is my London studio still holds hundreds of curated pieces — each being loved in a different way, for its abstract graphic hits of colour or tonal blends.

What started as a love of authenticity, materials, and archeology to a certain degree has developed into an ever-evolving experiment to play with patterns and colours in each of my collections which sometimes involves physically deconstructing original garments and reconstructing them as part of our "Remade in England" line and sometimes pushing to break the camouflage into individual elements, making each tonal island an artwork in its own right. Our latest collection is our most immersive experiment to date: taking inspiration from Ellsworth Kelly's deceptive, ground breaking and humorous ghost army to create a collection that aims to conceal, confuse and reveal in a playful and innovative experiment of deconstruction and reconstruction.

Of course what began with necessity for both man and machine has developed far beyond its origins. Camouflage today has become a ubiquitous urban language, covering a plethora of manmade objects with great effect. I've enjoyed charting these evolutions, immersing our world in a subverted counter-camouflage made of rich colours, bold graphics and an ever-changing flow of vibrantly impactful prints.

"I first became interested in camouflage not because of its inherent military link but for its playfulness — a subtle game of hide and reveal that takes so many forms."

Christopher Ræburn
Fashion designer

"There is something about the concept of shifting scales to change perspectives that really seduces me... On their own, these shapes represent imagined molecular landscapes where particles float around fluidly and the viewer is given a microscope to observe the world from a different angle."

Florence Blanchard
Painter, muralist & screenprinter

It is a great pleasure to be a part of Camo Mania, a wonderful and varied selection of camouflage from a wide variety of backgrounds. All of which demonstrate how such patterns have successfully made their way from their initial purpose as a defence mechanism in the natural world, into the equally complex arena of fashion, art and commerce.

Recurrent camouflage elements started appearing in my work over a decade ago. Somewhat subconsciously, I was making the transition from the familiar territory of graffiti lettering into the uncharted seas of abstract painting. And despite the shift of styles, these shapes not only bridged the gap coherently, they became a mainstay — either as standalone pieces or as a backdrop to more figurative and illustrative works. Currently, I enjoy painting large-scale murals and canvases as well as very small, more detailed works on paper — there is something about the concept of shifting scales to change perspectives that really seduces me. The versatility of this type of visual is particularly appealing when working with variable supports. On their own, these shapes represent imagined molecular landscapes where particles float around fluidly and the viewer is given a microscope to observe the world from a different angle.

Underpinned by a knowledge that all matter is made of particles — whether it be animal, human or mineral — my artwork aims to magnify what the human eye can't see. I aim to question our idea of visual perception. As a trained molecular biologist, I have thoroughly observed nature through powerful microscopic lenses and this experience has permanently affected my perception of the world. Through these observations I became fascinated by how reality may appear differently depending on the level of magnification, and how sometimes looking at something too closely may cause you to lose sight of the bigger picture.

When surrounding my figurative and illustrative work, these shapes represent an abstracted version of the natural world, in which changing angles, colours and scale can express a wide range of emotions and sets the overall mood of the piece. For example, creating dark and busy compositions with conflicting angles might help to express dynamic movement or impending doom. Whereas minimal compositions with brighter colours can represent inertia and joy.

Since I hand-paint the vast majority of my work, I have learnt not to underestimate the amount of stress which comes from the physicality of working outside. Not only are you confronted with questions and comments from passers or negotiating often adverse weather conditions, there are invariably logistical problems to overcome with each mural, such as a drainpipe in the middle of the wall, a branch that prevents you from using a ladder, or a cherry-picker that doesn't let you extend to the top corner and so on. Based on these variables, I have found it is best to remain flexible with the design and adapt accordingly.

Working with abstract, camo-like patterns provide me with a certain degree of confidence, as I know it is versatile and can fit in any number of circumstances, regardless of whether I am presented with a smooth, rough, large or small surface to paint. That said, this adaptable approach does make it near impossible for others to assist me, so despite the occasional help, I have to be involved in each step of the production, which can be physically challenging, but equally rewarding.

On the rare occasion painting isn't an option, the use of alternative media is a necessity and I am able to step away from production and watch the piece I have designed unfold. The work included in this publication is an example of such process. In this case I was asked by Museums Sheffield to create an artwork for Millennium Gallery's glass frontage.

The main requirement was that it lasts a minimum of two years. Vinyl graphics are one of the methods of choice for creating durable visuals in the public space. Indeed, painting on a transparent surface can be unflattering if you like bold colours, so utilising vinyl was the perfect opportunity to explore the refractory and reflective properties of glass, incorporating different colours, opacities and transparencies — so that's the option I chose, giving the artwork the intensity of a contemporary response to a stain glass aesthetic.

In order to transform the visual into vinyl, the design was converted into vectors and each shape was cut out of individual pieces of a specific colour. The project was particularly complicated as we couldn't apply any colour section in one go as they were simply too big. Creating numerous registration marks, we built up a background framework, which we could then insert more manageable sections into and build up the overall composition like a jigsaw puzzle. Luckily, I had a team of specialists to help with that part and the end result was a huge success – a big and bright hello to all Sheffield visitors as they entered the city from the main station.

Featured Artists & Designers: A-2-O Studio • Akatre • Aktiva Design • Apart • Asuka Watanabe • Atelier Neşe Nogay • Bethan Laura Wood • Bielke&Yang • Blok Design • BLOW • Carmen Nácher • Ching studio • Christopher Ræburn • Claire Bruining • Cobra Branding Studio • Domas Miksys, Aiste Jakimaviciute, Jone Miskinyte • Elsa Boch • Ercolani Bros., codice-a-barre • Estudio Campana • Fanny Löfvall, Nastassja Basekay, Oliver Sjöqvist • Fantasista Utamaro • Felipe Pantone • FILFURY • Florence Blanchard • Germán González Ramírez • Giovani Flores • Isabella Conticello • Janine Rewell • Jean-Yves Lemoigne • Jérôme Masi • Jess and Stef Dadon • Kitty McCall • Krizia Robustella • Laura Inat • Leanna Perry • Lee Ken-tsai • Lera Efremova • Les Graphiquants • Leslie David • Leta Sobierajski • Merijn Hos • Mirror Mirror • Monika Lang • Murmure • MWM Graphics • Naonori Yago • Nick Liefhebber • Olek • POOL • Quentin Monge • RISOTTO • Ronnie Alley Design • Sagmeister & Walsh • Shigeki Matsuyama • sstudio • Studio Feixen • Studio My Name is Wendy • Studio Toto • Susu Studio • Tobias Rehberger • Violaine & Jérémy • Wu Tzu-hung, Lin Yi-chen, Chiu Ping-song, Chou Chang-yung, Chen Yi-huang, Hong Shuo-yu • Yeye Weller

Oslo Design Fair 2016

BIELKE&YANG

Illustration: Sandra Blikås/byHands
Client: Oslo Design Fair

Twice a year, design industry leaders convene at the Oslo
Design Fair to exchange knowledge around Scandinavian
furnishing designs. The 2016 autumn version celebrated
"Togetherness" that spoke of closeness and warmth,
which Bielke&Yang acknowledged in a dynamic identity
co-developed with illustrator Sandra Blikås. A hint of
human-nature harmony characterised the pattern design
as a nod to Scandinavian designs.

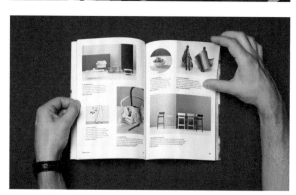

OSLO
DESIGN
FAIR

1—4
SEPTEMBER
2016

STØ
G E
SEN T
R E H

B-Boy & B-Girl by Alyssa Ashley

APART

Graphic design: Agra Satria
Client: Alyssa Ashey

Indulging the millennial taste for hip hop and pop culture, Alyssa Ashley's B-Boy & B-Girl Hip Hop perfume range arouses the senses of today's youth by unifying the idiosyncrasies that the two cultures have to offer. The perfume packaging fraternises luminescent colours and camouflage designs with rigid black and metallic patterns, culminating in a striking visual concept described as "Electro-Hip-Pop".

Samurai

**FANNY LÖFVALL, NASTASSJA BASEKAY,
OLIVER SJÖQVIST**

Client: Brobygrafiska

To connect Samurai's Japanese menu with a fun grown up crowd, the fictional restaurant's name and graphic identity visually point to the Asian country's culture. The project brief required student designers to submit an elaborate brand profile and propose a new takeaway model, and the solution unites Samurai's own brews, takeaway packaging and stationery with a colourful pattern mix. Achieving a strong brand presence, the design guarantees a delightful dining experience wherever it takes place.

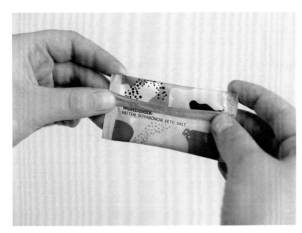

Bereza

A-2-O STUDIO

Client: Bereza

The primary function of Bereza's milling machines and the name (Russian for "birch") work their way into the workshop's logo with letters abstractly arranged to resemble tree bark. Several wooden logo signs composed of random cutouts were made to reflect the variety Bereza's products offer. Individuality was further reinforced with contrasting patterns adorning patterns through and through.

Memphis Collection

LAURA INAT

Decades after it emerged in the capital of Italy, Memphis continues to spread its influences today in Laura Inat's stationery design. True to the movement's iconic style, the geometric design was initially created with paper cut-outs and paint before being digitised for further use. A comparatively sedate palette gives the items an elegant, modern touch.

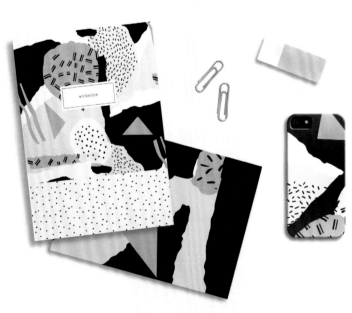

LUCIA MISHQUILA BRICHTA

SSTUDIO

Client: LUCIA MISHQUILA BRICHTA

LUCIA MISHQUILA BRICHTA's jewellery appreciates plasticity and natural forms. Created to coincide with the launch of her new collection made with dark recycled rubber, the brand identity and the announcement card utilise black, yellow and ragged shapes to unite elegance with handmade quality, like her jewellery does on the wearer's body. A clean logotype contrasts the irregular patterns which extend across tote bags and the designer's social networking site.

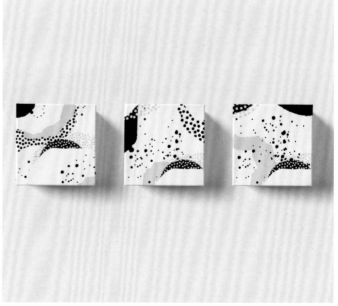

Dan Mladih 2015

MONIKA LANG

Client: ALTOM

Every year the city of Kragujevac in Serbia celebrates Youth Day with art workshops, movies, exhibitions and concerts. To engage young people with the day-long festival organised by youth centre, ALTOM, the posters visualised the dynamics of the varied programme in a flat, warm colour palette. Essential details of its day and night programmes were listed separately on the admission tickets with clarity.

"Here, patterns serve as a means to capture and convey a specific emotion, making the materials visually striking in a general sense."

Muro Festival Illustration

GIOVANI FLORES

On a graphic design assignment to promote a festive event at the student's choice, Giovani Flores chose Muro, a two-day music event in São Paulo. Carnival hues and brick pattern drawn from the Brazilian capital's tropical weather and cityscape overflow the posters, flyers and bags, and typify Muro's vibe. Botanical imagery, fauna, flags and faces give a solid clue of what to expect.

Liquid Dreams & Goede Papieren

NICK LIEFHEBBER

Client: (Liquid Dreams) De Dakhaas,
(Goede Papieren) Vruchtvlees, Literature Museum

Dream and reality blur in Liquid Dreams in response to
Utrecht-based magazine De Dakhaas' issue about the dark
hours. Psychedelic compositions awash with colours simulate
a sense of powerlessness and intense hallucinations that
emerge in one's sleep. On facing page, a set of three full-
page work illustrates the content of three literature pieces,
representing GL Durlacher's haunting memories of WWII, a
dialogue, and a feminist's thought.

PARCO Summer Fest at IKEBUKURO

ASUKA WATANABE

Art direction: Isu Taeko, NNNNY
Client: PARCO IKEBUKURO

Light-hearted, fun, and mood-lifting are three words that best describe the design for the 2016 Summer Festival PARCO. Visitors and passers-by were filled with awe when visiting this local Tokyo department store as its shop was decorated with a series of colourfully stunning illustration-led artworks including display ads, hanging banners, posters, and shop windows.

WORD. Open Air für die gute Sache

STUDIO TOTO

Client: Our/Berlin Vodka, Lemonaid, Notes of Berlin

On a mission to light up the grey urban neighbourhoods of Berlin for WORD. festival's benefit concert, Studio Toto upgraded the iconic camouflage patterns of Berlin's subway seats with a burst of spring-inspired colours. The visual identity's harmony of pattern and colour and use of a memorable self-made tape-font invigorate and prepare the city for its celebration of street art, music and poetry.

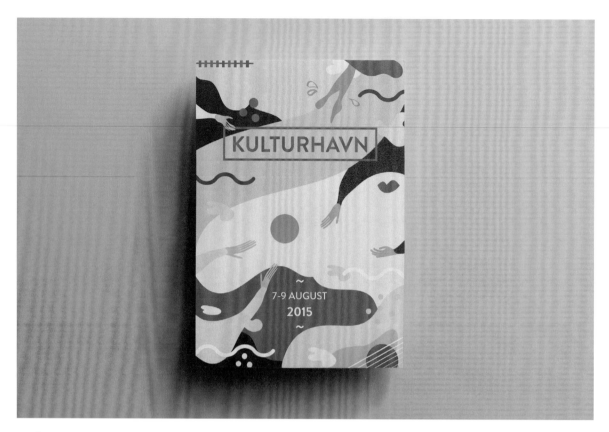

Kulturhavn 2015 Proposal

ISABELLA CONTICELLO

Copenhagen's Kulturhavn Festival is the largest harbour festival in Denmark. Every year the August event packs harbour areas with locals going for dance, music, watersports and harbour tours, which becomes a confluence of light summery colours and symbols that highlight cultural and ethnic variety. As water is central to the eclectic line-up, the posters and banners drew on free-form shapes to get viewers ready for a splashing good time.

CH Africa Limited Edition

AKTIVA DESIGN

Client: Puig for Carolina Herrera

Extracting fragrances from the land, Caroline Herrera's Africa Eau de Toilette conjures a sensory trip into the beauty of the African safari. Pairing camouflage patterns with golden accents, the brand portrays the glamour and luxury of the African spirit by evading the conventional European gaze and its tendency to exoticise. The identity's contrasting colours and imagery of giraffes and compasses altogether demonstrate that Africa's true essence lies in its fullness and richness of heritage.

"Patterns are everywhere. I find my inspiration in small details of everyday life."

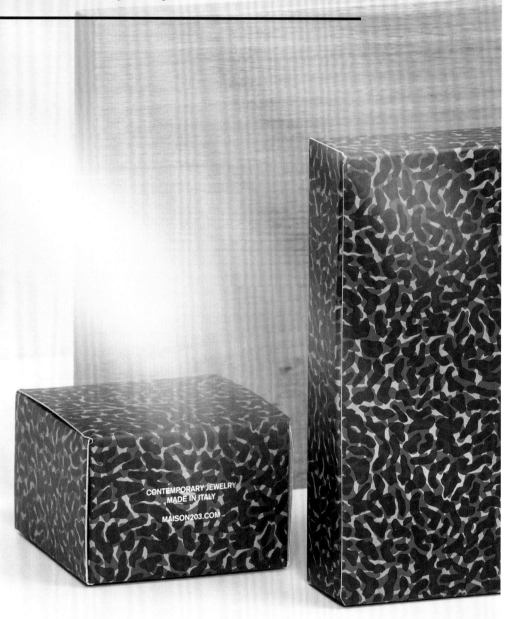

CONTEMPORARY JEWELRY
MADE IN ITALY
MAISON203.COM

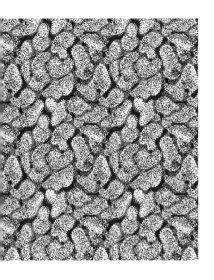

POOL pattern for Maison 203

ELSA BOCH

Photography: Ferréol Babin

Using camouflage-inspired patterns and layering translucent colours over each other, Elsa Boch's POOL patterns cloak the packaging for Maison 203's line of 3D-printed jewellery. Originally executed in watercolour, Boch's work was chosen and adapted for the Italian brand's collection. The fluid pattern is enhanced with a golden typeface, which adds delicacy and grandeur to the overall print.

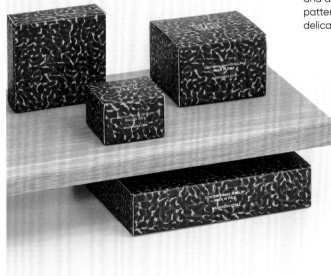

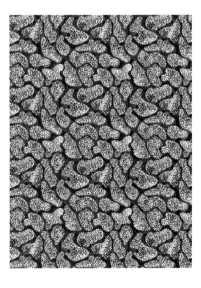

Melez Lifestyle Tea

ATELIER NEŞE NOGAY

Photography: Fevzi Ondu
Client: Melez Tea

To highlight the hand-crafted nature of Melez Lifestyle Tea, Istanbul-based Atelier Neşe Nogay opted for painterly patterns that echo the sophistication of the product. This limited-edition series packaging comes in refreshing colour combinations that not only represent the luxurious quality of the brand but also the distinctive taste and aroma of its fine teas and tisanes.

I'M UNCLEAN
A LIBERTINE AND
EVERY TIME YOU
VENT YOUR
SPLEEN I SEEM TO
LOSE THE POWER
OF SPEECH
YOU'RE SLIPPING
SLOWLY FROM MY
REACH YOU GROW
ME LIKE AN
EVERGREEN YOU
NEVER SEE THE
LONELY ME AT ALL

ANTIDOTE

CARMEN NÁCHER

A personal project comprises a series of three typographic posters. Designer Carmen Nácher played with proportion and communicated her aesthetic and an idea to use art as an antidote to stress and the complications of modern life. Using clean layout, minimal typography and subtle colour, the overall design is simple yet screams personality.

WITHOUTYOUI'MNOTHING

SUMMERHILL

MARKET

SUMMERHILL

MARKET

Baguette
Multigrain

$1.99

SUMMERHILL

MARKET

SUMMERHILL

MARKET

Summerhill Market

BLOK DESIGN

Client: Summerhill Market

Summerhill Market's new brand identity serves to enrich its reputation in Toronto as a local provider of extensive high-quality food products. The family-run business' progressive spirit and affable atmosphere are reflected in the cheerful and organic camouflage-patterned drawings. These raw and detailed patterns evoke the cruciality of craftsmanship, while monochromatic prints and minimalist labels maintain a sense of identity and continuity throughout.

FLUID ERA

WU TZU-HUNG, LIN YI-CHEN, CHIU
PING-SONG, CHOU CHANG-YUNG,
CHEN YI-HUANG, HONG SHUO-YU

FLUID ERA is an artistic production that articulates both the conflicts and convergences between two generations. Inspired by traditional Chinese landscape ('shanshui') paintings, each mountain represents a different generation, where separate streams flow and finally, after picking up momentum, converge within the same unifying pool of water. The different fragments of colour embody the ideas or perspectives belonging to each generation, elucidating both the individuation and coexistence of separate viewpoints.

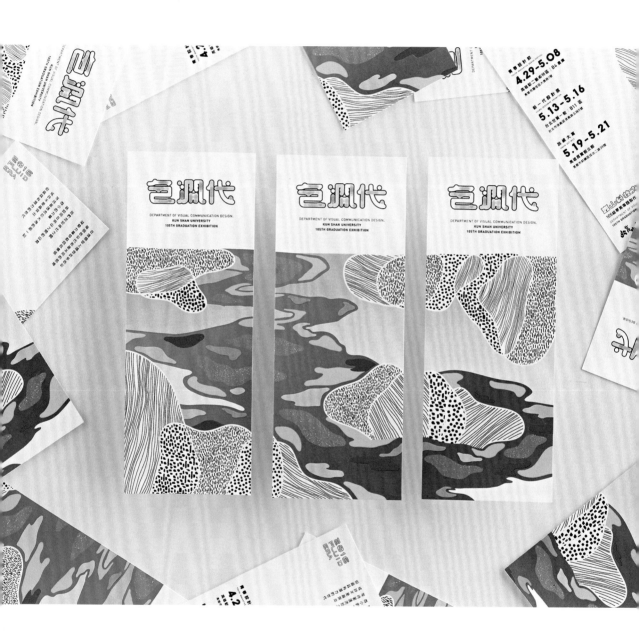

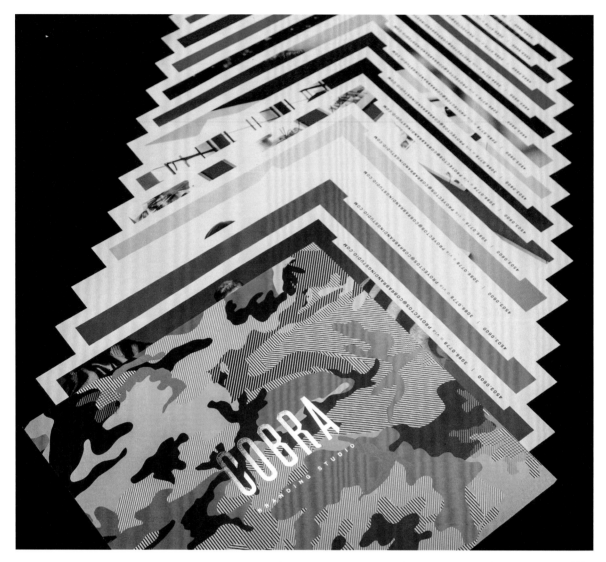

Cobra Brand Identity

COBRA BRANDING STUDIO

As evidenced by its name, COBRA is a creative studio that strives to enhance versatility by changing its skin and taking risks with every new endeavour. With a black, grey and hot pink palette that celebrates modern dynamism, the upgraded camouflage patterns indicate COBRA's audacious resolve to transcend traditional strategies of communication through their work.

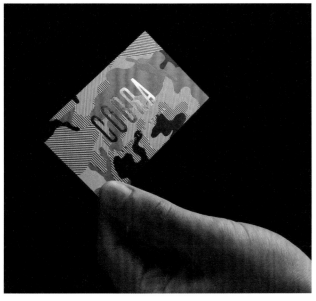

Moi

CHING STUDIO

Client: Department of Visual Communication
Design, Kun Shan University

"Moi" is all about pushing the boundaries
of what can be achieved via visual
experimentation. The design has opted to
represent movements in nature with fluid
curving lines and the gradient, metallic
swirls of red, green, yellow and blue,
demonstrating how to create a subtle yet
dynamic aesthetic through a typically static
design element – squiggle.

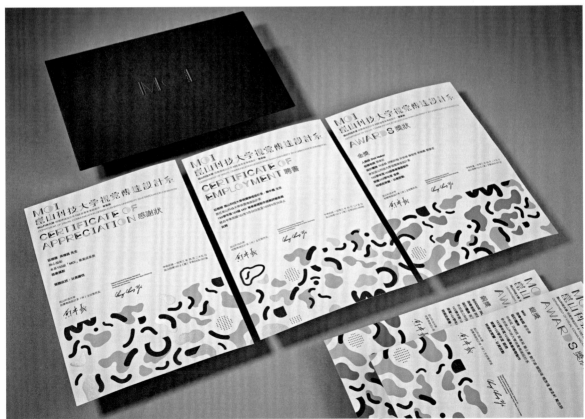

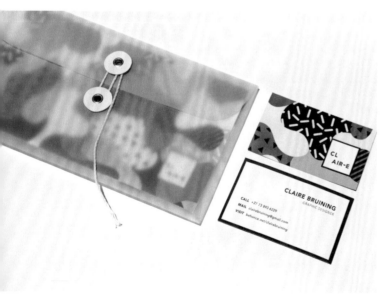

Claire Bruining Brand Identity

CLAIRE BRUINING

Graphic designer Claire Bruining decided to put a spin on traditional visual branding and developed identity components for her practice to reflect her refreshing approach to design. To give a boost to personality and inspire confidence in clients, Bruining incorporates clean typography with playful patterns, resulting in a cohesive personal identity that creates the impression of polished professionalism.

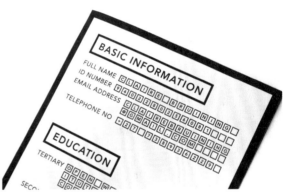

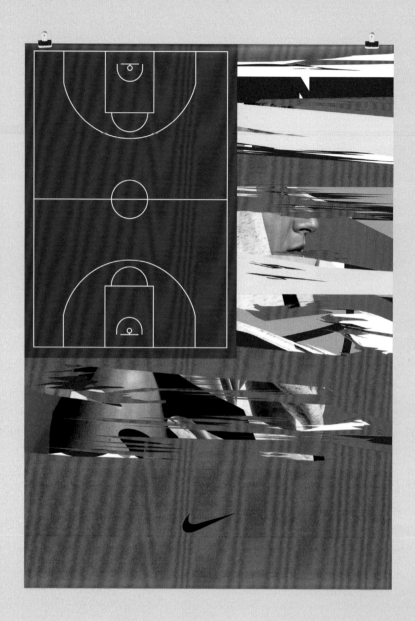

Bring Your Game

STUDIO FEIXEN

Client: Nike

Studio Feixen's collaboration with Nike Basketball for the Bring Your
Game campaign was all about conveying the right feeling through
design. Demanding the adrenaline and energy that comes with
playing basketball, the campaign's cryptic visuals arouse feelings
of spontaneity and curiosity. By experimenting with collage and the
effects of psychedelic camouflage patterns, the studio created a
refreshing visual language that agrees with the dynamism of sport.

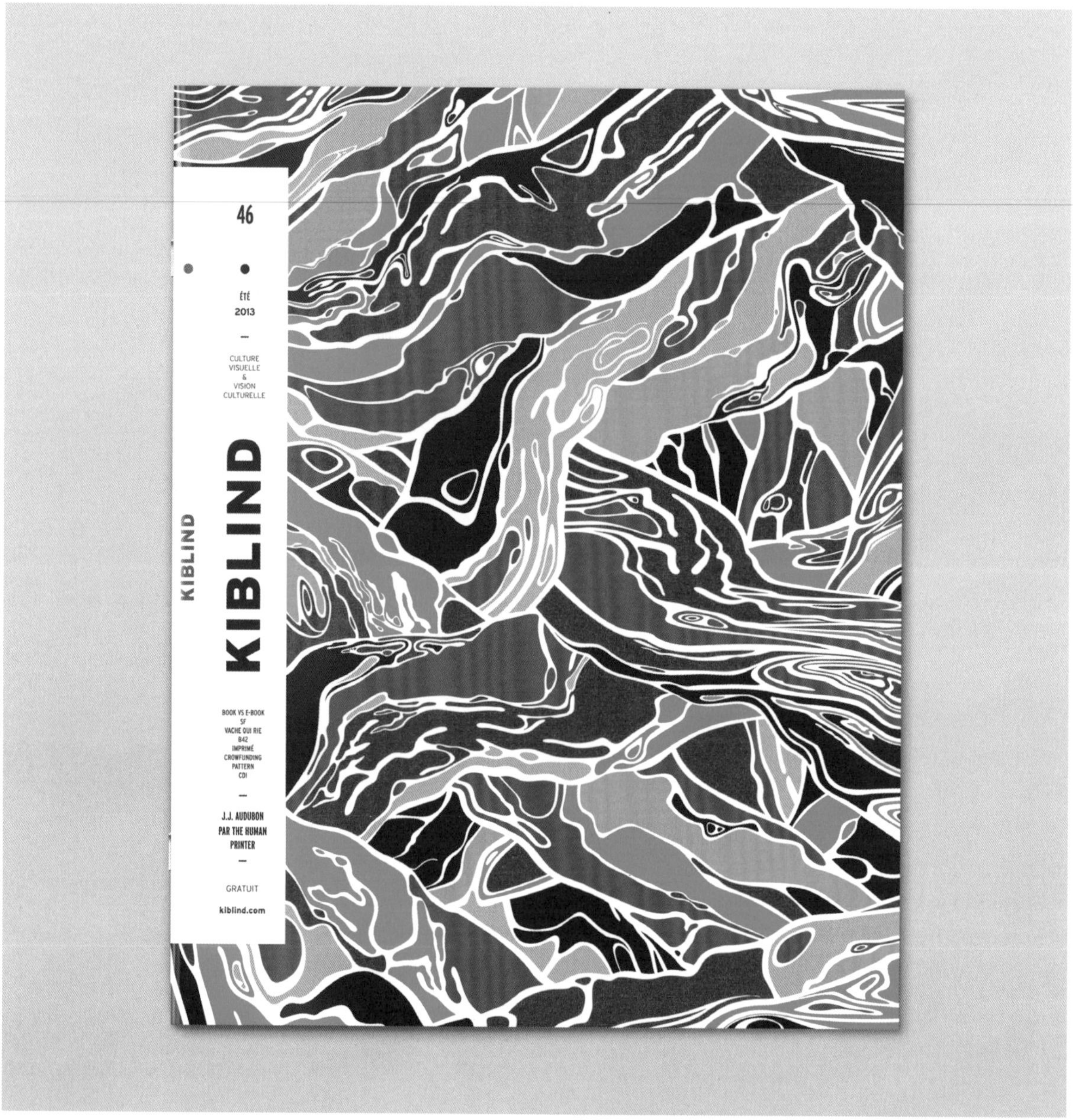
46
ÉTÉ
2013
CULTURE
VISUELLE
&
VISION
CULTURELLE
KIBLIND
KIBLIND
BOOK VS E-BOOK
SF
VACHE QUI RIE
B42
IMPRIMÉ
CROWFUNDING
PATTERN
CDI
J.J. AUDUBON
PAR THE HUMAN
PRINTER
GRATUIT
kiblind.com

Kiblind

STUDIO FEIXEN

Client: Kiblind

Visual arts and culture magazine, Kiblind, reached out to Felix Pfäffli of Studio Feixen to design the cover for their 46th issue. Pfäffli produced for the cover an interesting amalgam of colours, shapes and textures. The cover's surreal appearance began from the image of a piece of bacon, and through an exhaustive process of digital transformation and experimentation, he fabricated a mixture of aesthetic graphic patterns, effectually transforming the real into the unknown.

Vlow!

STUDIO FEIXEN

Client: Vlow!

A modular design which sees colourful bulbous forms flowing amongst linear typographic compositions, the identity for Vlow! Festival envisioned by Studio Feixen symbolises continuous motion and interaction. Drawing from the festival's emphasis on collaboration between speakers and audience members, the design's mingling of contrasting forms illustrates the crucially harmonious result of good communication.

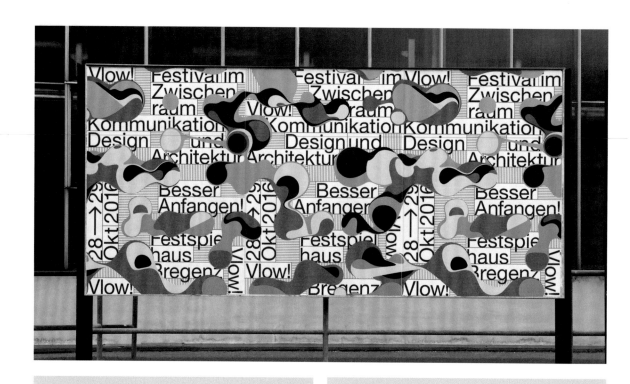

Festival im
Zwischen
raum
Vlow!
Kommunikation
Design und
Architektur

28 → 29
Okt 2016

Besser
Anfangen

Festspiel
haus

Vlow!

Bregenz

Ronnie Alley Design Brand Identity

RONNIE ALLEY DESIGN

Innovatively using the initials of her company to spell the word 'RAD' and playing with colourful geometric patterns, Ronnie Alley Design's brand identity simultaneously reflects Alley's own personal identity as well. His manipulation of chaotic patterns and a large colour scheme evoke a fun and friendly spirit that give the brand, and himself, a charming and personable energy.

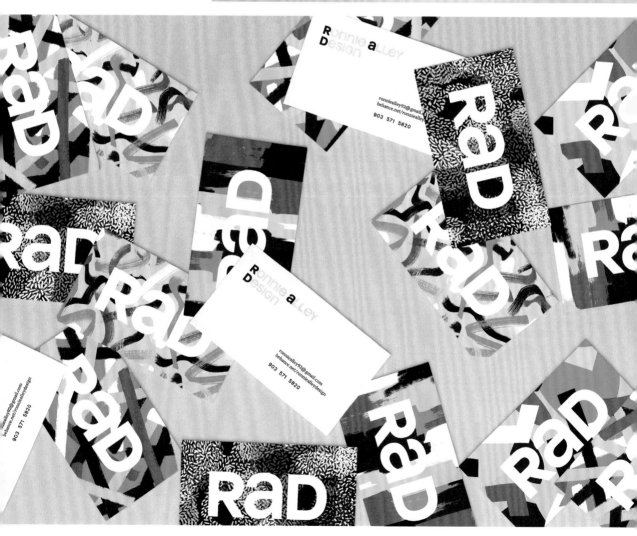

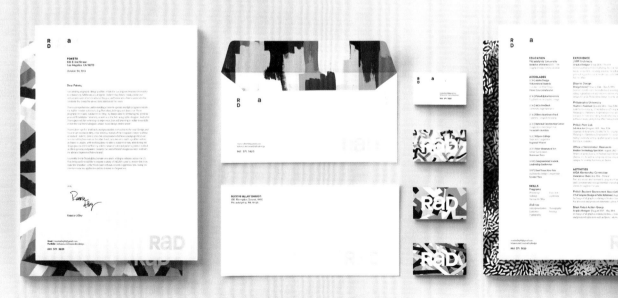

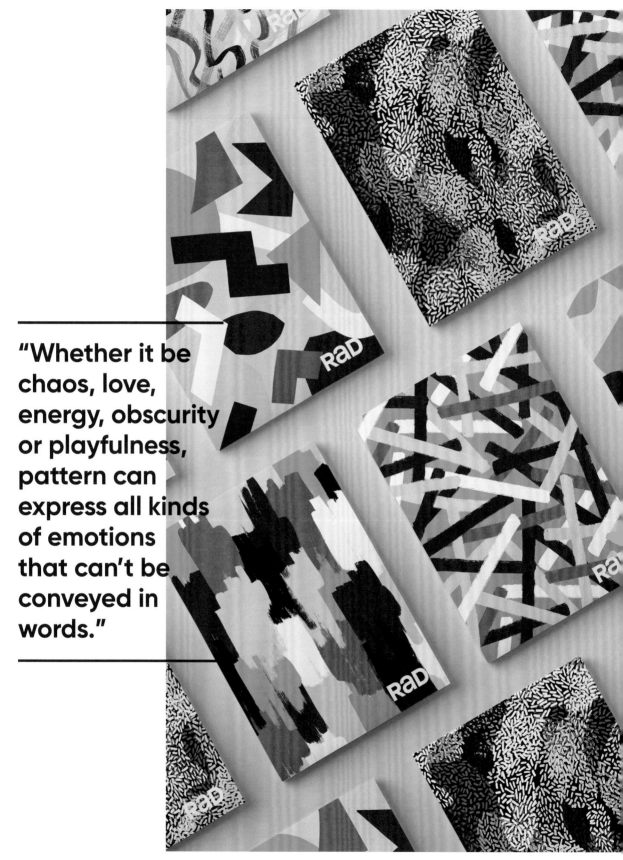

"Whether it be chaos, love, energy, obscurity or playfulness, pattern can express all kinds of emotions that can't be conveyed in words."

Toro Y Moi, Causers of This Album Redesign

RONNIE ALLEY DESIGN

Art and music often complement each other in bewildering ways. The cover art for musician Toro Y Moi's 'Causers of This' album strives to express the artist's concern with the causes and effects of a deteriorating romance. By disguising two figures beneath a muddle of disorganised colours and shapes, RAD's design envisages the confusion and ambivalence found in perishing relationships.

Camo Peoples

JÉRÔME MASI

Client: MAISON TANGIBLE

In response to MAISON TANGIBLE's 'L'interview timbrée', Jérôme Masi was tasked to design three stamps in a series called 'Camo People'. Inspired by the representation of stamps as universal symbols for interpersonal and cultural connections, Masi's illustrations aim to visualise the effacing of contrived borders between individuals, to represent humanity as a homogeneous and harmonious whole.

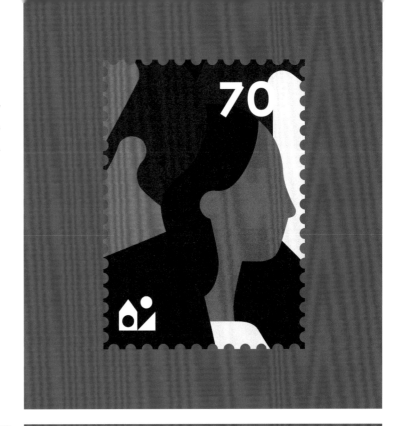

Women

QUENTIN MONGE

The celebration of women and femininity has never been a task that comes without contention. Quentin Monge and Jukebox Print's design for letterpress postcards depicts female figures in a camouflage facade. The cohesiveness and subtlety of the illustration turns our attention to a persistently undermined power of 'the weaker sex' and instead, invites us to recognise femininity as an indispensable strength.

Candy Chéri Love Box

QUENTIN MONGE

Photography: Samantha Kerdine
Client: Candy Chéri

Boxes of candy are a Valentine's Day staple; French luxury candy brand, Candy Chéri's Love Box celebrates both romance and sensuality in this playful collaboration. Illustrated by Quentin Monge, the boxes are teeming with male and female figures embracing life-size sweets and occasionally dressed provocatively. These flirtatious and tongue-in-cheek images brand the products with a seductive quality that befits the spirit of Valentine's Day.

What's Next? 2014 Visual identity

**DOMAS MIKSYS, AISTE JAKIMAVICIUTE,
JONE MISKINYTE**

Photography: Greta Gedminaite
Client: What's Next conference of creative industries

'What's Next?' is a Lithuanian conference that celebrates the advancement of globalisation and human innovation. The abstract patterns of bright colour found in their identity not only embody the playfulness and dynamism of the brand but allude to the conference's use of colour-coding as a form of visual communication. This, along with animated icons and a simple upward spiral logotype, add functionality and serve to convey a message of modernity and never-ending world change.

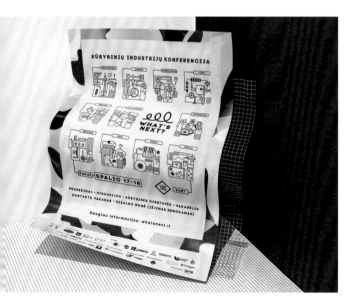

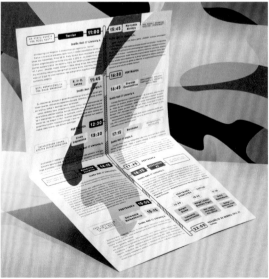

L'atelier du savon 2014 AW

NAONORI YAGO

Client: AMBIDEX
Special credits: SIX inc.

The L'atelier du Savon clothing line for adults harnesses a playful and nostalgic spirit that caters to the personality of every individual. Naonori Yago's identity for the brand channels the theme of nature. Adding to the reflections of the beholder's surrounding off the mirror surface, Yago borders photographs of models in woodlands with brown, yellow, green and blue camouflage patterns. The typography for the brand mimics the clumsy handwriting of a toddler, recalling for adults the innocence and gaiety that comes with childhood.

Full Brow Cosmetics

SUSU STUDIO

Photography: Nogani Moore
Client: Full Brow Cosmetics

Boldly ignoring familiar visual trends and striving for a new and unique direction, Susu Studio's design for Full Brow Cosmetics features ambitious original artwork. Throwing in vivid hues and wild patterns, the brand identity does away with the period's mainstream penchant for minimal packaging and instead, through a distinctive approach, attracts the attention of a larger demographic.

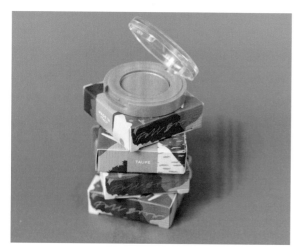

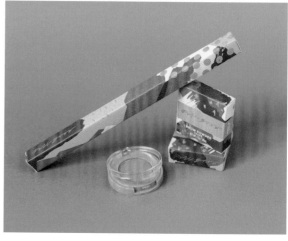

Vélo Velo

POOL

The name 'Vélo Velo' combines the French word for bicycle and Italian word for scarf, respectively. This wordplay intends to be reflected in the brand's products, which are scarf designs inspired by the world of cycling. One of their designs features a vivid camouflage print with a small racing flag in the middle and halftone patterns, which are often found on bicycle frames and sportswear.

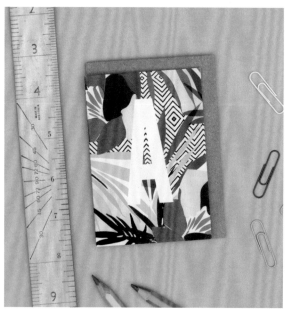

TROPICALIA Type

KITTY MCCALL

With twenty-six designs for each letter of the alphabet, the Tropicalia card prints by Kitty McCall draw upon the 'tropical' theme in a striking and fashionable way. McCall juxtaposes large multicoloured flower graphics with black-and-white patterns and a contemporary typeface, altogether decorating a bold nature-inspired aesthetic with an urban twist.

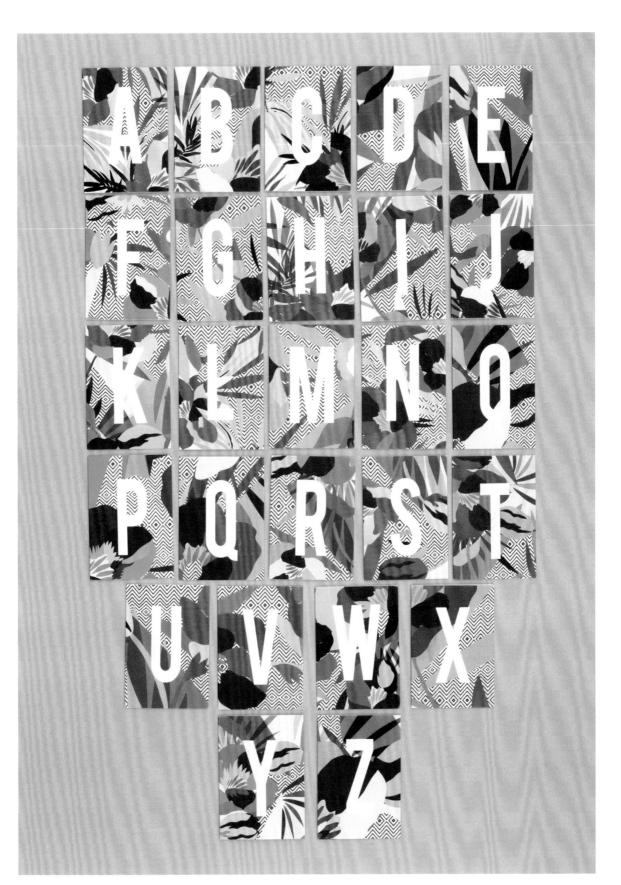

LANDSCAPE

KITTY MCCALL

Inspired by the foliage and mountainous imagery of Henri Rousseau's jungle paintings, Landscape by Kitty McCall incorporates nature's elements in a geometric style and with an overwhelmingly green colour palette. With the intention of making each upholstered piece of furniture display a different pattern, Landscape is designed asymmetrically and in abstract proportions. McCall plays with small- and large-scale patterns to create diversity and a sense of depth for the beholder.

KITTY McCALL INTERIOR TEXTILES PRINTED IN THE UK

KITTY McCALL INTERIOR TEXTILES PRINTED IN THE UK

TROPICALIA

KITTY MCCALL

Drawing from the familiar designs of the Tropicalia prints, Kitty McCall's Tropicalia textiles similarly combine modern and floral styles. Blooming in exaggerated proportions and vivid colours, these floral patterns are inspired by Georgia O'Keeffe's enlarged flowers and Andy Warhol's floating flowers. By continuously layering each other, the bold floral designs and monochromatic patterns unify both pastoral and urban elements.

OneGroove

YEYE WELLER

Client: OneGroove Records

In search for an artwork that veers from the usual minimalist design of electronic and house music, German record label, OneGroove, decided on something more unique and eye-catching. The disorganised camouflage pattern and use of undulating shapes offer an eccentric quality to the artwork. Each release manifests a different colour scheme that adds character to the work and ultimately makes it more recognisable.

Super Kolor

YEYE WELLER

Yeye Weller's Super Kolor series experiments with the properties of colour and balance. As a visual study of the relationship between the two, Weller's work attempts to achieve aesthetic harmony by playing with various layouts, colour palettes and composition. Beneath its disordered facade, Super Kolor is a meticulous dissection into the characteristics of good design.

"It's all about balance — the right ratio of light to shadow, objects to white space, and lighthearted elements to the formal ones."

SUPER
KOLOR

Molecular Landscapes

FLORENCE BLANCHARD

An observant and perceptive muralist, painter and screenprinter, Florence Blanchard's diverse artworks take a meticulous interest in the scientific elements that make up our world. Supported by her passion for molecular biology, Blanchard aims to continuously challenge our comprehension of reality through various art mediums and magnified perspectives. As such, through the versatility of camouflage patterns, she conducts visual studies on the fluidity and structure of molecular landscapes — the unfamiliarities of which confront viewers with startling and insightful windows into the world.

1.

1. Dust, 2015. Painting on canvas. Private commission

2. 1993, 2014. Acrylic on canvas. Produced for 'Wu Tang is for the children' exhibition in London.

3. Topsy, 2016. Mixed media sculpture. Produced for The Children's Hospital in Sheffield.

4. Der Biochemische Zyklus, 2015. Acrylic and gold leaf on canvas. Produced for The University Of Sheffield. Photographed by Andy Brown.

2.

3.

4.

5.

6.

7.

5. Particles, 2012. Street Collage. Curated by W49 in Brussels, Belgium.

6. Kodama, 2014. Mural. Personal project in Bekkai, Hokkaido.

7. Particles, 2015. Mural. Curated by Yuck Print House in Manchester, UK.

8. Particles, 2015. Mural. Personal project in Sheffield, UK.

9. Particles, 2013. Mural. Personal project in Sheffield, UK.

8.

9.

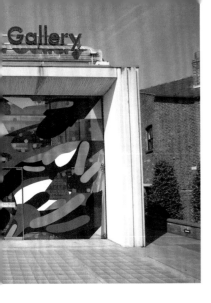

Particles

FLORENCE BLANCHARD

Photography: Andy Brown
Client: Millennium Gallery Museums Sheffield

Inspired by the indispensability of particles to all matter, Florence Blanchard's window vinyl graphic for Millennium Gallery Museums imagines the appearance of magnified particles. Drawing from her experience as a molecular biologist, Blanchard plays on the refractory capacities of different types of vinyl on a window and their subsequent effects on interior space. The scale of this 'molecular' design instigates questions about reality and the various perspectives in which we can view it.

We Love Green Festival 2016

LESLIE DAVID

Client: We Love Art

The urgency of environmental protection and sustainability has become ever-present in today's climate and Paris' WE LOVE GREEN festival aims to promote these exact values. Leslie David's visuals for the event feature distorted and psychedelic landscapes that portray mountains, rocks and rivers. The dream-like quality of the patterns perceives the natural world as infinite and ethereal, conveying a message about the substantiality of nature and our communal responsibility for it.

FESTIVAL

WE LOVE GREEN

MUSIC ART TALKS FOOD NATURE

SAMEDI	DIMANCHE
4	**5**
JUIN 2016	JUIN 2016

LCD SOUNDSYSTEM
PJ HARVEY
AIR
DIPLO
PNL
HOT CHIP
AMON TOBIN DJ
HUDSON MOHAWKE
FLOATING POINTS
FKJ
KELELA
ÂME
L'IMPERATRICE
FATIMA YAMAHA
SUPERPOZE
JACQUES
& MANY MORE TO COME

BOIS DE VINCENNES, PARIS

PRÉVENTES SUR
WELOVEGREEN.FR & FNAC.COM

#WLG2016

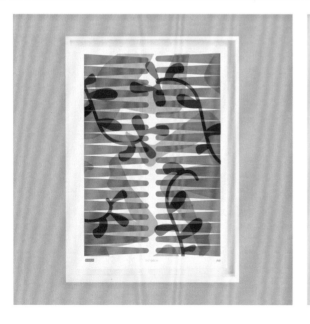

104

RISOTTO Product Collection

RISOTTO

The RISOTTO Product Collection includes mini calendars, card and print collections, notepads and beach towels, all decorated with colourful risograph patterns. The risograph technology allows for the layering of colours and shapes, giving these tropical designs an added charm. With a blend of geometric, polka dot and foliage patterns, these compact products carry with them a sense of zest and eccentricity.

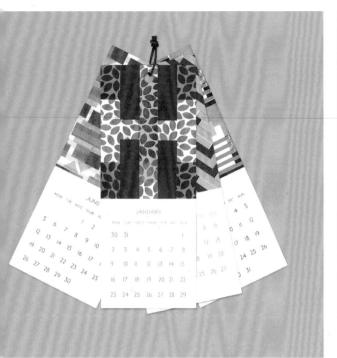

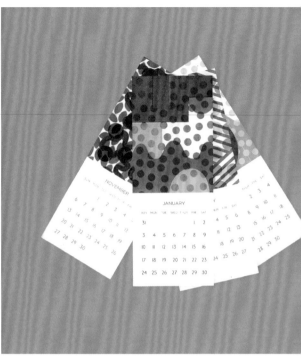

Collage it!

LERA EFREMOVA

Replete with diverse patterns, colours and shapes, Lera Efremova's 'Collage It!' series adorns greeting cards, stickers and other decorative items with a festive and charming mood. Juxtaposing monochromatic segments with colourful ones, and complex patterns with plainer ones, Efremova moulds and interacts disparate portions with each other to culminate in a single unified design. By confronting the eye with these uncanny relationships, she mirrors the essence of those found within nature.

108

name

phone

email

web

If you dream it, you can do it.

CELEBRATE
THE LITTLE
THINGS

TEAROOMCAFE

AUGUST 28
2017 2:00 PM
TEAROOMCAFE
M A
— you & me —

BE HAPPY,
BE BRIGHT,
BE YOU.

Outstanding Chinese Typography Exhibition 2014 Visual Identity

LEE, KEN-TSAI

Design: Lee Ken-tsai, Suri Cheng, Cheng Yang-chun, Lee Wonhan
Layout: Hsiang Jou-hua

Identifying with the function of his project, Lee's visual identity for his Chinese Typography Exhibition envisions a personal and playful take on Chinese typography. Filled with textured strokes and warm colours, the designs portray various characters in a carefree style, set against a chequered ensemble of jumbled patterns. The enthusiasm of his visual identity works to electrify the exhibition and admire the art of typography.

"Patterns I designed are always functional and identify with my projects. You can read, feel, and easily understand what they represent."

Lugard Visual Identity & Packaging

BLOW

Client: Lugard

Championing wildlife animal protection and poverty in South Africa, Hong Kong quality food store, Lugard, embraces the visual concept of an African Jungle. The brand's identity glorifies the themes of nature, safari and animals by incorporating bright primary colours and lively imagery. Their mascot is a cheetah named Lugard, who represents excellence, superiority and vigour — altogether encompassing the atmosphere they aim to bring to their customers.

JUNGLA Agencia publicitaria

GERMÁN GONZÁLEZ RAMÍREZ

Client: JUNGLA Agencia publicitaria

As a window into the world behind their name, publicity agency JUNGLA's visual identity aims to embody a refreshing and youthful vibe through a wildlife theme. Inspired by the jungles of South America, the brand's graphic system engages with a combination of camouflage patterns, textures and animals. Striving for optimal visual impact, colour selection plays a crucial role to these visuals, which depend significantly upon an appropriate balance and interaction of shades.

Down the Rabbit Hole 2017

MERIJN HOS

Client: Mojo Concerts / Live Nation

This phantasmagorical experience of Merijn Hos' design for Down The Rabbit Hole 2017 once again revamps the Dutch festival's identity with an elevated sense of magic. The infusion of colour gradients, vector-based patterns, globular and plant-like shapes contribute to the visuals' surreal and mysterious quality. Hos explores with form, structure and composition to create a psychedelic aesthetic that complements the festival's celebration of the arts.

Mercedes Benz Mixed Tape 62

MERIJN HOS

Client: Mercedes Benz

The cover art for the Mercedes–Benz Mixed Tape 62 strives to capture an ultimate summer mood. Satiated with a wacky interaction of globular shapes and exuberant colours, the abstraction reminisces the musical works of illustrious artist Wassily Kandinsky, whose paintings visualise the experiences of sound and sight. The illustrator, Merijn Hos, described the image as an evocation of the feeling of driving fast with an open window.

"Patterns can be like music. They feel and look consistent but are not necessarily repetition. They are easy on the eye and can take you away for a minute."

Untitled by **MERIJN HOS**

Portrait

AKATRE

Client: Nameless

The cover art for French music group Nameless' 'Portrait' EP plays with the effects of camouflage by blending a woman's face with her surroundings. The band's contradictory name signifies their desire to transcend boundaries by prioritising the sound of their music over a prescribed epithet. This intention to move beyond conventions of identity is conceptualised through camouflage, where concern for the human subject is diluted and the patterns and colours are foregrounded.

Integrated 2015

MIRROR MIRROR

Web development: Matthias Deckx
Client: Integrated, Sint Lucas Antwerpen

Integrated provides an essential platform that stimulates dialogue between art, design and society. The conference invites speakers to compare and share their work, leaving behind a sense of 'indigestion'. The visual identity for their 2015 event incorporates black-and-white illusory patterns that fold and melt into each other. The enthralling and bemusing quality of these visuals conceptualise the nature of Integrated, which through a meeting of artistic figures, leaves attendees feeling speechless and overcome.

En attendant Nördik Impakt

MURMURE

Client: Arts Attack!

In preparation for the pre-event to the annual electronic music festival 'Nördik Impakt', Arts Attack! was asked to design a powerful visual identity that would excite music lovers for the event's 18th anniversary. Consistent with the festival's strong monochromatic logo's layout and typeface, the pre-event identity is equally impressive, illustrating a surreal turmoil of worm-like patterns that are akin to optical illusions.

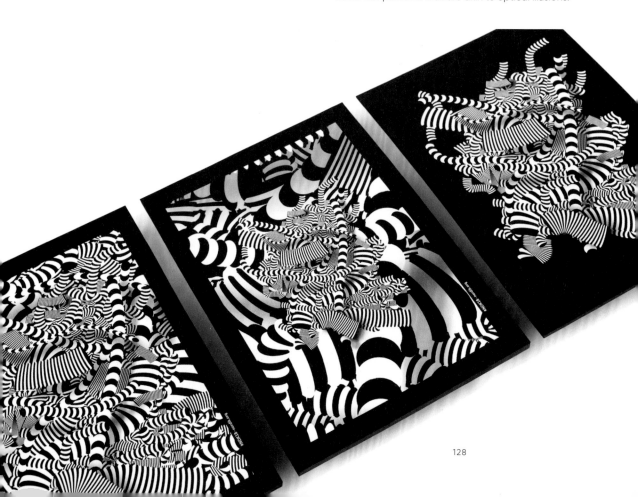

Within the poster: ART3, 30 ANS / ART3, ÉDITIONS, A, R, T, 3, ART3, ÉDITIONS, ART CONTEMPORAIN, 3, 0, EXPOSITIONS, A, RÉSIDENCES, ÉDITION, N, ART3, WWW.ART3.ORG, 30 ANS / ART3, S, IMPRESSION / DESIGN GRAPHIQUE : MY NAME IS WENDY

art3 — 30th anniversary

STUDIO MY NAME IS WENDY

Art direction : Sylvie Vojik
Client: art3

My Name is Wendy created a visual identity for art3's 30th anniversary that reflected its timeline of exhibitions, productions, residences and more. This concept of temporality is visualised in 16 posters that are composed of repeated graphic modules, which through digital adjustments in opacity, movement and proliferation, develop into a successive layering of shapes. Dedicated to all the people who have worked with art3, the series illustrates the state of travelling and living within the authority of time.

JCDecaux

art 3
art contemporain

30 ans - Exposition du 23 février au 11 mars 2017
du mercredi au samedi de 14h à 18h - Entrée libre
Vernissage jeudi 23 février à 18h30 | **8 rue Sabaterie** contact@art-3.org

VILLE DE
VALENCE

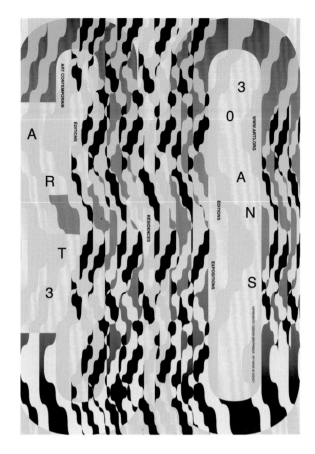

"There are insertions within layers that create micro-differences in density and transparency. This principle stages a 'ghostly' module and creates a temporality through the succession of areas or surfaces."

Poolhouse Rock / Canal St. Martin / Autumn Foliage Series / Snorkel Camo

MWM GRAPHICS

Within the city of Nantes and Paris in France, and Montreal and Boston, an ongoing series of spray-painted murals colour the streets. The murals admire the natural world through portrayals of its organic and stimulating geometries. These handsome pieces of art visualise the energy and beauty of free-flowing water, molecular structures, woodlands and more through the use of camouflage patterns, brilliant colour schemes and rhythmic imagery.

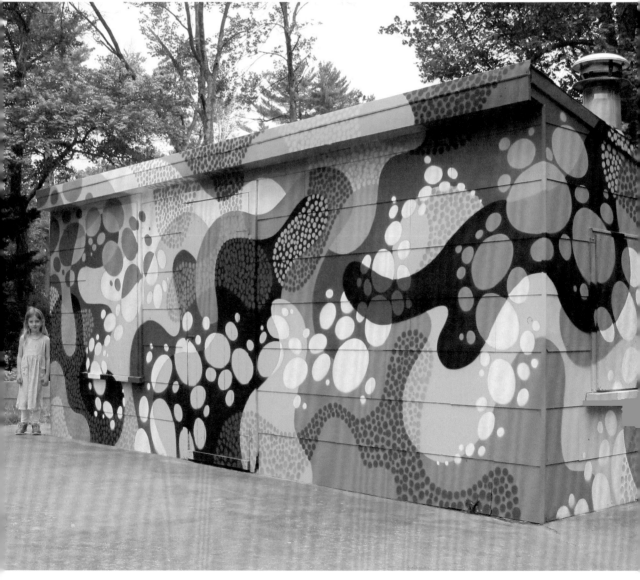

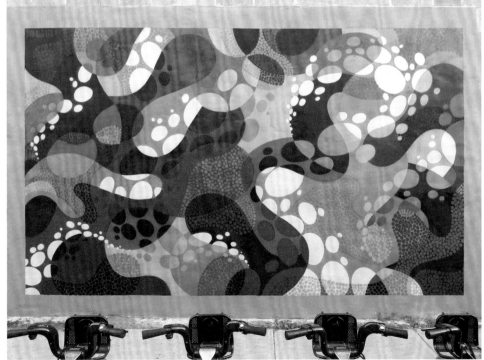

135

The Train That Stands Still

OLEK

As an individual consistently relocating herself, Olek is fascinated by the concepts of movement and transformation, exemplified particularly in the form of locomotives. Having crocheted bicycles, cars and even people, crocheting a massive steam-powered train provided the opportunity not only to reanimate a bygone relic but also to continuously transform viewers' perceptions. Intrigued by the unrelenting connection between street art and trains, Olek equally makes her mark on the world through 'acts of madness'.

How Two Live x Buffalo
for Print All Over Me

JESS AND STEF DADON

Special credits: Print All Over Me, Buffalo

Taking on an ambitious project that celebrates a love for over-the-top prints, shoe brand Buffalo and fashion bloggers How To Live refresh the fashion of camouflage clothing at the time of release. Infusing a blend of pastel and vivid colours, and recalling the trend of 90s platform shoes, the collection proves both modern and nostalgic, completing an impressive style that pushes boundaries.

144

Life is Beautiful Festival

FELIPE PANTONE

Curation: Just Kids Official
Client: Life is Beautiful Festival

From his beginnings as a graffiti artist, Argentinian Felipe Pantone took his talents to the streets of Las Vegas for the city's Life is Beautiful festival. He transformed a white building's facade into a futuristic mural replete with kinetic patterns, 3D shapes, glitch imagery and abstract geometric proportions. The contrast between his monochromatic background and the jolting colours of the foreground produce an electrifying 3D effect that excites the senses.

MCM x Tobias Rehberger

TOBIAS REHBERGER

Client: MCM HQ
Courtesy: neugerriemschneider Berlin, MCM

Amalgamating his own penchant for monochrome and geometric patterns with the strong logo branding of MCM, artist Tobias Rehberger developed a line of bags that feature robust and pervasive stripe prints. The flagship store fuses product with architecture in a theme called "If you want the rainbow, you gotta put up with the rain". This title refers to the act of revealing something camouflaged within a chaotic sculptural space of optical illusions.

"I've been particularly interested in this paradox of creating a visual art project which was about 'not seeing something' and at the same time uses bold geometric shapes and sharply contrasting colours. Dazzle painting for me perfectly represents this paradox. It is geometry-based and therefore can be applied differently to architecture."

149

Narcissism : Dazzle Room

SHIGEKI MATSUYAMA

Artist Shigeki Matsuyama has created a room-sized
installation in which a person disappears into lines, curves
and zigzags that crash beautifully against each other. This
optical, patterned playground is a sharp-witted mixed media
art piece that questions our identity in the age of social
media where the boundary between self and self-image is
unconsciously blurred.

MINNA
PARIKKA

MINNA PARIKKA

JANINE REWELL

Photography: Jonas Lundqvist
Bodypainting: Riina Laine, Saara Sarvas
Client: Minna Parikka

Using the human body as a canvas marks a profound moment when life begins to imitate art. Janine Rewell's advertising campaign for Finnish shoe brand, Minna Parikka, paints graphic art onto the female body to camouflage her. The geometric patterns and dynamic poses complement and draw attention to the design and colour of the shoes worn. Rewell's captivating and seamless photo compositions transform human beings into instruments for art – the ordinary into the extraordinary.

Frooti Fizz

SAGMEISTER & WALSH

Photography direction: Zak Mulligan
3D art: Pablo Alfieri, Pierre Bourjo, Sagmeister & Walsh
Retouching: Daniel Plateado, Ekaterina Markevich
Special credits: Nadia Chauhan (Parle Agro CMO)
Client: Parle Agro

The advertising campaign for India's first mango fizzy drink, Frooti Fizz, features Bollywood actress, Alia Bhatt. With eye-catching optical illusions, zestful colours and a surrealist aesthetic, the quirky campaign brings a refreshing energy that matches the drink's bubbly and revitalising quality. The large illusory patterns enliven and stimulate the senses, culminating in a bold and assertive brand identity.

M·A·C Camouflage

LEANNA PERRY

Client: M·A·C Cosmetics

Creatively combining camouflage patterns with digital collage, the poster series for M·A·C Cosmetics melds the artistry, beauty and energy of the brand. Taken from the AW17 Fashion Week, the posters interlace photographed beauty looks, fashion textiles, makeup products and vivid colours. The camouflage structure allows the brand to reveal glimpses of their virtuosity, seductively enticing viewers with glamorous looks and products.

Print All Over Me Collaboration

LETA SOBIERAJSKI

Photography: Tom Neal
Styling: Courtney Cho
Hair & makeup: Amy Chin, Model: DJ Smith / Major Models
Client: Print All Over Me

Print All Over Me's free online platform for budding fashion designers enables creative talents like Leta Sobierajski to grace the fashion world with refreshing clothing designs. Having painted the patterns herself, Sobierajski's patterns are infused with various combinations of white, blue, black and red colour swatches. The integration of some giraffe-inspired and camouflage patterns give the clothing eccentricity and liveliness, perfectly embodying PAOM's principles of collaboration and creativity.

Da Lazer Room

KRIZIA ROBUSTELLA

Photography: Dizy Diaz, Lidia Juvanteny

The Fabrica Moritz factory in Barcelona, Spain, was filled with hip-hop music and B-boys breakdancing during the opening event for Krizia Robustella's capsule collection. Inspired by a similar scene in the comedy movie, Ali G Indahouse, Da Lazer Room features eye-catching multi-coloured camouflage tracksuits that cater to contemporary adolescents' enthusiasm for hip-hop culture.

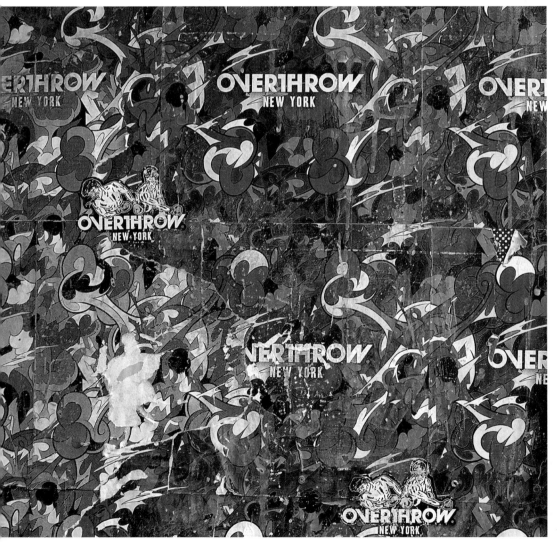

Group Show 'Daily Routine', at Overthrow Boxing Club NYC

FANTASISTA UTAMARO

As a special collaboration with NYC's Overthrow Boxing Club, Fantasista Utamaro designed a pair of fight gloves and boxing trunks characterised by an omnipresent skull and a disruptive cloud pattern. Titled 'Pirate Skull', the artwork visualised 'liberation', wishing that everyone in the world could enjoy greater freedom as they should. His illustration was put on display in an art group show 'Daily Routine' held at the club as posters sprawling across the venue's facade and punching bags to achieve an overall anarchic and retro aesthetic. A-Chan and LP also participated in the show.

"'Pirate' symbolises 'challenge' and hence, indicates 'challenge freedom' in this series, the freedom that exists in everybody's history and circumstance."

The Legend Of Pop Culture Install Series 01

Fantasista Utamaro

'Yankii' culture represents a long-standing and influential faction of Japanese society often criticised for their rebellious and arrogant social behaviours. Inspired by a character from the manga, *Bukkomi no Taku*, who rides a motorcycle to school, The Legend of Pop Culture Install Series features two women dressed in striking clothing sat atop an equally decorated motorcycle. Using camouflage patterns and masks to denote the suppression of Yankii culture, Utamaro makes a controversial statement about Japan's social tendency to stigmatise unwonted and free-spirited individuals.

Mangacamo

FANTASISTA UTAMARO

At the heart of Tokyo's culture is the famous crossing in front of Shibuya station, where over one million people pass by everyday. Fantasista Utamaro envisions this daily scrambling of people in the form of a camouflage pattern. Replacing individuals and objects with indistinct shapes, manga-style bubbles and onomatopoeic words, he embraces the irreplaceable atmosphere of commotion and excitement inherent to Tokyo. The design extended to a jumper the artist co-created with Mikio Sakabe, which Masami Nagasawa wore for magazine *What's a Fantasista Utamaro*'s cover shoot done by Yoshiharu Ota, as shown on facing page.

"The pattern I made means imagination, desire, fantasy and life to me. It never ends unless you crop it with a frame. The multiplication keeps going if you want it to."

Cut and Paste
Capsule Collection

KRIZIA ROBUSTELLA

Photography: Cesar Segarra

The collaboration between Lauro Samblás and Krizia Robustella for the 'Cut and Paste' capsule collection visually combines the designers' creative styles. Samblás' signature layering of geometric shapes and Robustella's carefree and hyperactive designs enmesh in the clothes' manifestation of superimposed images, camouflage patterns and overall 'cut and paste' style. The freedom of these design techniques are enhanced by the garments' sporty and casual style, producing an invigorating aesthetic.

AMI JUNGLE

VIOLAINE & JÉRÉMY

Client: AMI Paris

In honour of AMI's S/S 2014 collection, illustrators and graphic artists Violaine & Jérémy designed a tropical jungle print that would be perfect for spring and summer. Permeating shirts, trousers, baseball caps and duffel bags is a photo-realistic colour pencil drawing of foliage and flowers. With lots of shading, texture and accents of bright colours, the overarching print maintains a remarkable authenticity towards natural imagery.

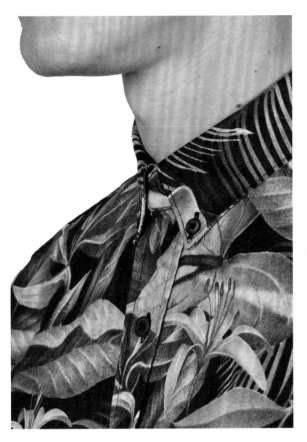

SS17 MCM x
Christopher Ræburn

CHRISTOPHER RÆBURN

In celebration of the brand's 40th anniversary, MCM collaborated with renowned designer, Christopher Ræburn, for a ready-to-wear collection that recalibrates the relationship between sustainability and luxury aesthetics. Designed for the modern-day nomad, Ræburn enmeshes MCM's iconic Cognac Visetos monogram within a geometric Jacquard camouflage print that recalls his signature militaristic style. The range adopts the likes of Schoeller textiles along with Ecocalf Nylon made from recycled water bottles.

Black Street

KRIZIA ROBUSTELLA

Photography: 080 Barcelona Fashion

Krizia Robustella's FW 2016/17 collection, Black Street, features monochromatic clothing decorated with Nicasio Torres' watercolour portraits, and faux fur coats in striking camouflage patterns. Inspired by the 1980s' streets of New York, Robustella's deluxe sportswear collection attempts to break the stereotypes of black culture by combining luxury and streetwear aesthetics, which encapsulate a rejuvenating take on New York's suburban hip-hop scene.

AW17 Eastpak x Christopher Ræburn

CHRISTOPHER RÆBURN

AW17 and Eastpak's exclusive collaboration implants the authenticity of Ræburn's sartorial language onto Eastpak's functional backpacks. The three-piece capsule collection of bags, made from 100% recycled and reused fabrics, produced an innovative patchwork that harmonises sustainability and functionality. By juxtaposing repurposed camouflage patterns with the fluorescent detail from border force uniforms, the collection establishes on a playful and exciting take on 'Remade' fashion.

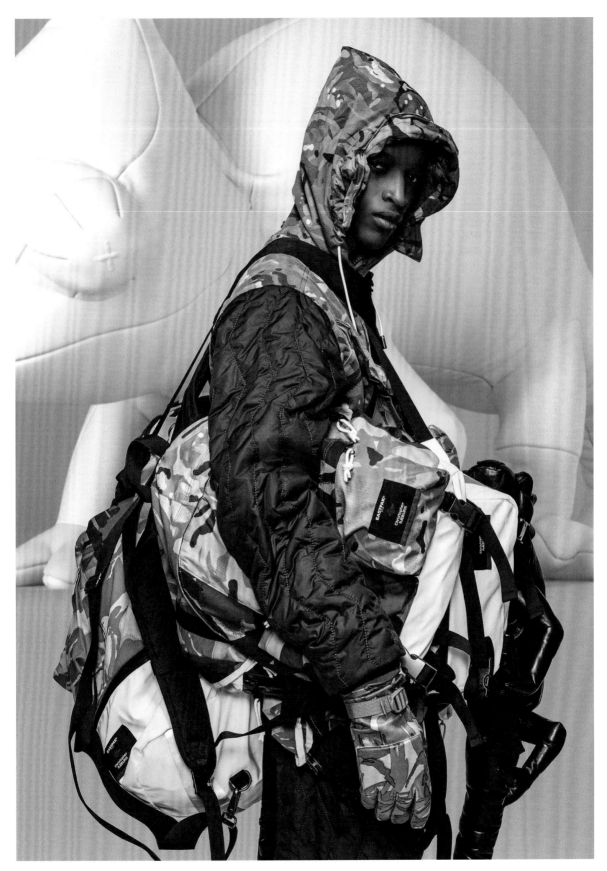

187

Christopher Ræburn
AW17 CUT N' SHUT collection

CHRISTOPHER RÆBURN

Through the process of deconstruction and reconstruction, AW17's CUT N' SHUT collection experiments with the brand's REMADE, REDUCED, RECYCLED ethos. Inspired by abstract artist Ellsworth Kelley's deceptive and thought-provoking 'Ghost Army' hoax, Ræburn equally aims to conceal, confuse and reveal with this collection of coats and biker and bomber jackets. Repurposing materials from bomb disposal uniforms, blankets and camouflage jackets, AW17 authentically reconstructs the concept of camouflage-inspired fashion.

Black Rainbow Camo Series

JEAN-YVES LEMOIGNE

Art direction: Julien Gosset
Vegetal styling: Alice Auboiron
Hair & make-up: Jean Pierre Canavate
Casting: Maud Cosials
Client: Black Rainbow Magazine
Special credits: Jay Smith

Having been asked to choreograph a design spread for the outdoor issue of Black Rainbow Magazine, Jean-Yves Lemoigne wanted to take on a more imaginative direction. Instead of venturing outdoors to photograph a blending with nature, he decided to bring natural motifs indoors, set against the plain white backdrop of the studio. The project involved matching graphic patterns with wild organic ones and styling them in a photo series that brought out the best in camouflage design.

191

192

"It was an attempt to find a natural element that matches those graphic designs. Patterns represent the wild nature here."

Camo Windbreaker Skull

FILFURY

Production: Marie Kirkby

By deconstructing a Nike windbreaker and reconstructing it into a human skull, British artist FILFURY reified his love for camouflage patterns as a conceptual art piece. Rendered in a muted navy and mustard pattern with a slight sheen, the skull subtly ties street culture with nature, life and death. While the jacket's zipper and drawstring were taken to complete the form, they also whisper their original functions together with the prominent Nike logo.

"Patterns hold energy and life. They can dance and disguise. In my work, they give objects texture, life and identity. Visual cues to belonging. But mostly powerfully they give life to a surface."

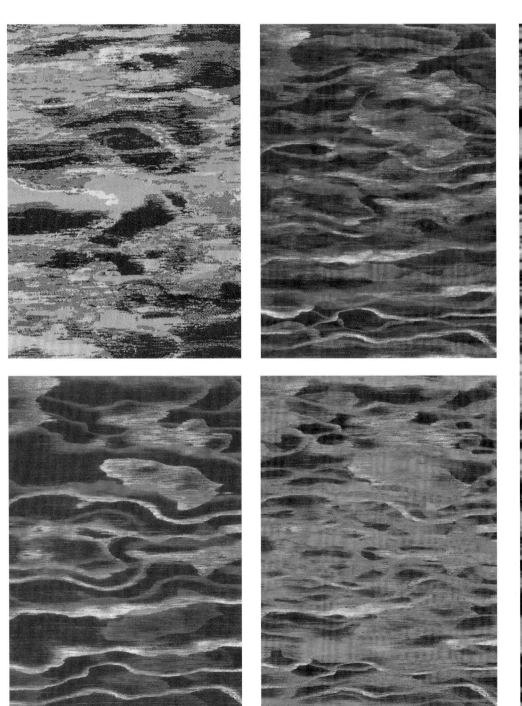
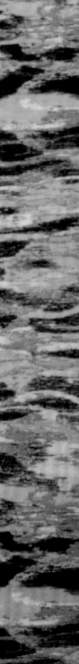

LCS R900 Cloud Jacquard

LES GRAPHIQUANTS

Photography: Maxime Tétard (pattern), le coq sportif
(sneakers)

What began as a research of patterns built on plywood sheets had become dashing artworks adopted by le coq sportif for their 2016 Spring/Summer retro-running collection. Nacreous colours and overlays of drawings result in a fluid pattern, evocative of evening clouds laced with iridescent light and, hence, the name "Cloud". Fusing vegetable and mineral to colour the wood gave the surface an impressionistic appearance.

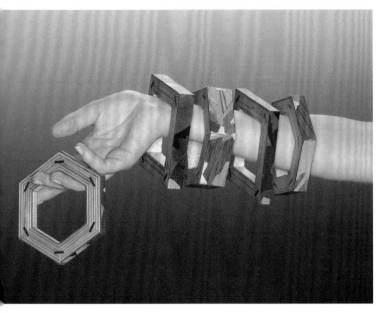

Particle-Jewellery

BETHAN LAURA WOOD

Photography: Ellis Scott

Using the leftover materials from Particle Furniture, this collection of bracelets and necklaces has developed into a set of companion pieces to the household fixtures. Each piece of jewellery is a slice from a hexagonal or square master extrusion, and the prominent streaks of black on the bracelets are naturally brought through by the tough insert. As each slice will have its own distinct marquetry surface, the outcome of the jewellery cannot be entirely controlled, making every piece idiosyncratic.

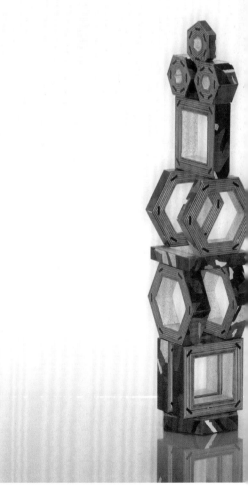

Particle-Stack

BETHAN LAURA WOOD

Photography: Ellis Scott

Inspired by the old shipping and warehouse complex, Butler's Wharf, Bethan Laura Wood's Particle Stack furniture system, with its interlocking and stacking units, is based on the design of crates and packaging materials. Her signature reappropriation of wood laminates mimics the textured patterns found on particle boards, raising a 'low quality' material into an eye-catching adornment. Through her experimentation with materials and techniques, Wood's Particle Stack is an organic and original take on modern furniture design. Particle is sponsored by Abet Laminati.

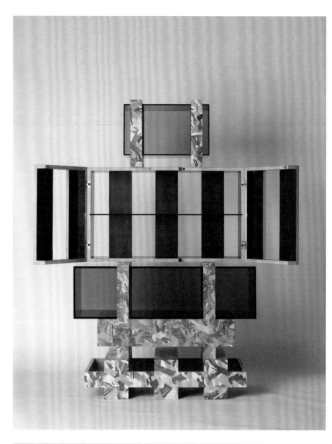

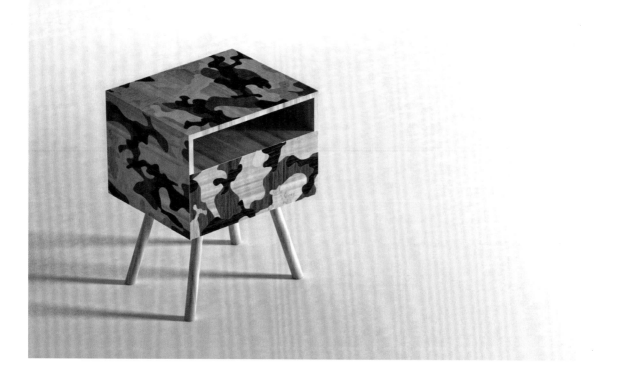

Guerrilla

ERCOLANI BROS., CODICE-A-BARRE

Client: BER s.r.l.

A collaboration between Italian design studio Ercolani Bros. and Alessio Gismondi of codice-a-barre, Guerrilla features decorative markings in a pale woodland palette. Drawing on a laser-cutting machine, the designers revitalised the intricate wood inlaying technique and rendered a camouflage pattern by piecing wood panels together. The filmy colour coating gives away natural wood grains and colours, and enhances the shelves with texture and warmth.

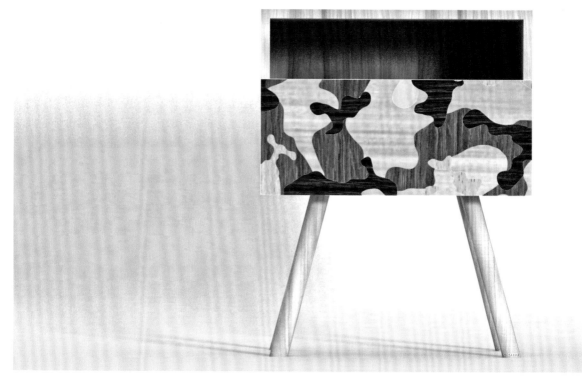

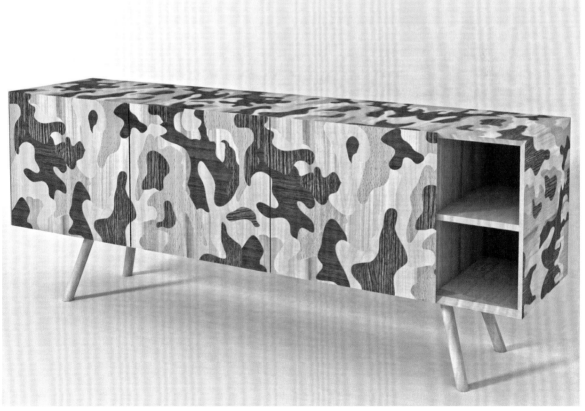

205

Aquário I

ESTUDIO CAMPANA

Client: BD Barcelona Design

Aquário I's language of design is based on the bringing together of contrasts and dichotomies. Inspired by aquariums, The Cabinet is a visual meeting of glass and solid wood, which denotes immateriality and physicality, cold and warmth. Cooperating wood or stained pine together with coloured glass is also functional; the transparent glass patches on the exterior and internal shelving allow light to pass through, while an opaque wooden framework gives the cabinet robustness, overall creating an enigmatic facade.

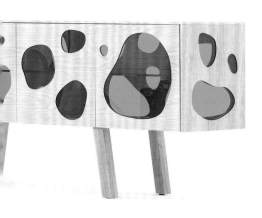

"Camouflage is all but epidemic now — it has gone viral, worldwide. We're in the eye of a camouflage storm. It's everywhere, in everything: in art, fashion, advertising, even in arcane proposals for doctoral dissertations."

Roy R. Behrens
Professor, University of Northern Iowa

Camouflage

Camouflage is all but epidemic now—it has gone viral, worldwide. We're in the eye of a camouflage storm. It's everywhere, in everything: in art, fashion, advertising, even in arcane proposals for doctoral dissertations.

The current attention that camouflage gets—in print, online, or wherever—is unprecedented. At the same time, there is a porous interplay between camouflage and the arts (meaning both fine and vernacular arts) that is not unique to our time period. Nor did we originate it.

As for the practice of camouflage, we cannot know when that began. There are amazing examples in the widest range of natural forms (including fossil evidence), and, as part of nature, presumably humans made use of it from the very beginning. How else could people have survived, both in escaping from predators, as well as in their search for food? Throughout history, there are recorded uses of camouflage in hunting or in waging war; recall the famous Trojan Horse, or Shakespeare's reference to Birnam Wood in Macbeth, in which soldiers were disguised as trees.

Modern Origins

A far more pragmatic question to ask is when did camouflage "as-we-know-it" begin, and that can be answered by tracing it to the 19th century. The subject came to prominence in the second half of that century, when it was used in attempts to confirm (or to disprove) the Darwinian theory of natural selection. Back then, it was known as "protective colouration" or "concealing colouration." It was not until World War I that it acquired the name camouflage, a French slang term that had to do with theatrical disguises and the duplicity of criminals.

To be fair, there were on-going discussions about appropriate field service uniforms, both prior to and early in WWI. There were some concerns about the blazing "red coats" of the British and the equally bright red trousers of the French, and eventually these were replaced by khaki (or dust-coloured) fabric, horizon blue or (in the case of the Germans) field-gray uniforms. But camouflage was not a major worry until the early days of WWI, when the technology of concealing oneself during warfare suddenly had to dovetail with advances in surveillance. And of course that arms race hasn't stopped—and it never will. Face recognition, invisibility cloaks, and drone surveillance; these are simply the latest examples of that.

Roy R. Behrens

Roy R. Behrens is professor of art and distinguished scholar at the University of Northern Iowa, where he teaches graphic design and design history at the University of Northern Iowa. Among his books on camouflage are *FALSE COLORS: Art, Design and Modern Camouflage* (2002); *CAMOUPEDIA: A Compendium of Research on Art, Architecture and Camouflage* (2009); and *SHIP SHAPE: A Dazzle Camouflage Sourcebook* (2011). His blog at camoupedia.blogspot.com has been described as "the most important online resource for anyone interested in the subject of camouflage." His most recent book is *Frank Lloyd Wright and Mason City: Architectural Heart of the Prairie* (2016).

Other issues were also beginning to surface at the end of the turn of the century. In researching animal camouflage, for example, it was claimed by some that artists, who had been trained to "fool the eye," often had a better grasp of how natural camouflage works than scientists. One of the groundbreaking books on the subject was produced not by a scientist, but by an American artist-naturalist, Abbott Handerson Thayer (now frequently referred to as "the father of camouflage") and his son, artist-naturalist Gerald Handerson Thayer (the book's author of record). Their ambitious masterpiece, made even more remarkable by the inclusion of their own full-colour paintings, was titled *Concealing Colouration in the Animal Kingdom: An Exposition of the Laws of Disguise Through Color and Pattern; Being a Summary of Abbott H. Thayer's Discoveries*. After years in preparation, it was released to wide acclaim in 1909, with a revised edition in 1918.

Abbott H. Thayer's findings about animal camouflage had appeared in scientific journals as early as 1896. In his initial articles, he claimed he knew the reason why a preponderance of animals have lighter colouration on their undersides, with darker colouring toward the top. At some point, because of his art school training, it had occurred to him that this kind of animal colouring is the exact opposite of shading, a technique fundamental to drawing and painting. Appropriately, his discovery became known as reverse shading or countershading. He and every artist knew that a flat two-dimensional shape can magically be made to look solid and three-dimensional—to appear to stand out from the surface—by colouring it lighter on the top and increasingly darker toward its base. These days, everyone does this—not just artists—whenever they use what is now called a "drop shadow" while working on a computer.

More simply, when an animal has "white undersides" (Thayer's term), its colouring tends to cancel out or counteract the shading produced by the overhead sun. As a result, whenever a person walks in the woods, and unexpectedly comes upon a deer, a bird or a rabbit—or nearly any creature that is active during daylight—at first that animal may seem flat, less solid or less thing-like, providing of course that it "freezes" (as do most instinctively) since the slightest movement will give it away.

When first proposed by Thayer, countershading was well-received, and it is still widely accepted today. Encouraged by his trespass into science, Thayer conducted outdoor demonstrations at scientific meetings in the US, the UK and in Europe. In advance of these, he installed on the meeting grounds handmade duck decoys, some of which (painted in a single earth tone) were immediately visible, while others (which he had carefully countershaded with light undersides) were not visible to the audience of scientists beyond a modest viewing range.

2

3

In the interest of finding a practical lucrative use for his research, he countershaded a replica of the Venus de Milo, using electrical lighting, so that, by alternating between light switches, the sculpture would appear or disappear. He also toyed with various ways of making an actor appear and not appear on stage, using artificial lights and countershaded body suits.

Wartime Applications

Early in WWI (the US had not yet entered the war), Thayer offered his expertise to the Allied armies. Among his observations was that khaki-coloured uniforms (although preferable to red coats) were ineffective camouflage. If the colour of the fabric was an unbroken continuous tone, it actually increased the visibility of the soldier, because of the shading produced by the sun. In contrast, Thayer argued (unsuccessfully) that the continuity of the uniform should be disrupted or broken up. Ironically, at about this same time—although Pablo Picasso and Thayer were unacquainted, and Thayer was all but dismissive of styles of so-called Modern art—Picasso apparently jokingly said that the most effective camouflage for the French infantry would be to dress them in harlequin costumes. It was Picasso's assumption that the disruptively coloured diamond designs would make the soldiers hard to see.

Returning momentarily to the years before the war, it is essential to realise what was happening in Germany around 1910, a year that marked the founding of a new style of psychology, called Gestalt theory. Its founders (Max Wertheimer, Kurt Koffka and Wolfgang Köhler) were especially interested in the psychology of perception. Their plans were interrupted by the outbreak of hostilities, but after the war, when they resumed working together, they made important advances in their research of human vision. They identified inborn tendencies that largely determine how camouflage works (a subject they mentioned repeatedly in their writings).

They did not fully know it then, but those same tendencies (or organising principles) also influence arrangements in art, architecture, fashion design, and page layout in graphic design. A decade later, an especially insightful psychologist (Angeline Myra Keen) pointed out that the Gestaltists' "laws of perceptual organisation" are in fact all but identical to Abbott H. Thayer's "laws of disguise." Like Thayer, in their references to camouflage, the Gestaltists stressed the distinction between disruption or "high difference" camouflage, and blending or "high similarity" camouflage.

It is interesting that when the first major international exhibition of avant-garde art (now commonly known as the Armory Show) opened in New York in 1913, the public responded by joking about how apparently disruptive the artworks were of the Cubists, Futurists and others. One work was famously described as "an explosion in a shingle factory." Like high difference camouflage, Cubist and Futurist artworks were chaotic and bewildering, and more generally, as critic Katherine Kuh wrote later in *Break-Up: The Core of Modern Art* (2014), new art of that era was "characterised by shattered surfaces, broken colour, segmented compositions, dissolving forms and shredded images."

Influence and Confluence

As for WWI, remember that it started just one year after the Armory Show. Early in the war, artists in the French infantry proposed that they should be assigned to camouflage. They demonstrated that cannon and field artillery teams were less detectable from an airplane if their shapes were broken up by high contrast abstract patterns. Not surprisingly, those confusion patterns looked a lot like Cubism and Futurism—but of course they also resembled a harlequin's outfit (aha!), crazy quilts, hidden picture puzzles, and the patchwork of the earth itself when viewed from the air. So, it is hardly surprising that people assumed that avant-garde artists at that time were somehow involved in inventing disruptive camouflage techniques. That said, it is ironic that, of the thousands of artists who served in WWI as camoufleurs (as they were then officially known), only a few were in sympathy with Modernists in civilian life. Rather, the vast majority were "commercial artists": portrait painters, illustrators, cartoonists, set designers and architects. Nevertheless, throughout WWI and ever since (there's no stopping it), a causal link is commonly claimed between Cubism and camouflage.

Other approaches to WWI camouflage looked like other styles of art, not just Cubism. For example, there was a commonly-used technique called "umbrella camouflage" (favoured by academic artist Solomon J. Solomon, who was initially in charge of WWI British camouflage) in which nets (comparable to fishing nets), interspersed with scraps of cloth, were suspended overhead. Because of the overhead sunlight, the shadows of these garnished nets were cast on whatever was below them (not unlike Andy Warhol's self-portraits in which camouflage designs were projected on his face), whether artillery, vehicles or personnel. It was an expedient way to disrupt shapes without having to paint them.

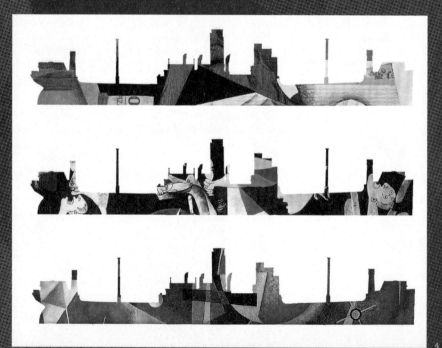

4

But even that was not without precedence. Prior to WWI, all sorts of painters (particularly Impressionists, as in John Singer Sargent's The Hermit (1908), or Breakfast in the Loggia (1910)) were shattering shapes using shadows. And the same device was also used effectively in experimental turn-of-the-century photographs.

Dazzle-Painting

If shape disruption was widely used in ground camouflage, it was even more effective in WWI naval camouflage, for which it was given the curious name of "dazzle-painting." That particular method was proposed in 1917 by a British marine painter and poster designer (hardly an avant-garde artist) named Norman Wilkinson. It came about because the requirements of ship camouflage were different from those of ground camouflage. At sea, viewing conditions are forever changing and there is no reliable background with which a foreground object might blend in. It was Wilkinson's wise admonition that the goal of camouflaging a ship was not to make it hard to see, but to make it hard to hit.

Dazzle-painting relied on blatantly contrasting schemes that made use of perspective distortions (called forced perspective), like the spatial illusions in theatre sets. But dazzle was almost exclusively used on merchant ships that were vulnerable to attacks by menacing German submarines (called U-boats). Specifically, it was designed to thwart the calculations of a torpedo gunner, who was peering through a periscope from a distant submerged submarine, in a wide range of weather conditions.

Today, one hundred years after dazzle-painting was adopted by the British Navy, we know quite a lot about how these dazzle schemes were made. In recent years, newly unearthed documents have been located in British and American archives. We know, for example, that the painting schemes were originated by male artists, not by women. When women did participate (in other than secretarial roles), they were typically assigned to building scale-model wooden ships, or, in some cases, to applying hand-painted camouflage schemes (provided to them by the men) to the ship models. These painted models were then taken to an observation theatre, where, one by one, each camouflaged model was tested to determine the extent to which its distortion scheme would throw off the directional estimates of experienced naval personnel. These were observed through a periscope under lighting and background conditions that replicated those at sea.

In attacking a ship, a U-boat gunner did not aim directly at the ship itself; he aimed at a spot ahead of the ship, in the hope that the ship and torpedo would intersect in time and place. To calculate that, certain information was essential, and the ship's course or directional path was especially critical. According to Wilkinson, if the directional estimates of those who were testing the models were off by eight degrees or more, there was a good chance that the torpedo would miss the ship. At the end of the war, when camouflaged ship models were tested under laboratory conditions at the MIT Department of Architecture and Marine Engineering (in a testing theatre used during the war), the worst directional estimates were off by as much as sixty degrees.

Public Enchantment

To artists and designers, there are few things as beguiling as WWI dazzle-painted ships. They are comparable to butterflies, or exotic colourful plants. We have thousands of black and white photographs of ship camouflage from that era, but, unfortunately, there are no colour photographs—not even one—since colour photography at the time was limited to Autochrome Lumiere, and apparently none were photographed. Some test models have survived (especially in British museums), as have paintings of the ships made by war artists at the time. The most revealing artifacts are several hundred coloured lithographic plans of the dazzle schemes that were used as guides in painting the ships (housed in the collections of the Imperial War Museum in London, the US National Archives and Records Administration, and the Fleet Library at the Rhode Island School of Design).

During the war, access to the dazzle plans was restricted. But the public did see camouflaged ships, if usually incidentally while traveling overseas or while they were moored in a harbour. Spit-and-polish naval personnel thought such ships were as tawdry as street walkers—they called them "Jezebels" and "tramps." To journalists, they were an amusing, welcome return to the hilarity of the Armory Show. They called the dazzle-painted ships "cubist paintings on a colossal scale," "a futurist's bad dream," "a floating art museum," and "a flock of sea-going easter eggs." One pundit said they looked like "a Russian toy shop gone mad."

As for the public, they fell in love with the colourful ships. By the final year of the war, there had been a profusion of dazzle costume balls, civilian boats and vehicles adorned in optically dizzying stripes, and (most popular of all) dazzle-painted bathing suits. In no time, the fascination with dazzle-painting became a public preoccupation, a camouflage mania like our own.

Even the military conceded to the camouflage craze. Taking advantage of the seductiveness of dazzle, the US Navy began to apply disruptive schemes to everything, not with the intention of hiding anything—but rather as a colourful way to rally the public, to bolster wartime fundraising and patriotic morale, and to replenish enlistments. For example, in July of 1918, the Women's Reserve Camouflage Corps applied a riotous camouflage scheme (a plan provided by men, of course) to the USS Recruit, a wooden recruiting station in the shape of a ship, built on dry land in the middle of Union Square in New York.

That same month, one of the floats in the Fourth of July parade in New York featured a small-sized dazzle-painted ship, positioned on a flag-like wildly coloured base. The use of dazzle-painting as advertising was a great success, and, thereafter, "tanks, ambulances and trucks were camouflaged at the request of different branches of the government to encourage recruiting, for wherever the [women] camoufleurs went in their uniforms, spreading their bright paints, a crowd was sure to gather."

After the War

Some of this camouflage frenzy eased as the war ended, in part because government funding declined or was redirected. In postwar UK, unemployed navy veterans were hired to work in concession stands in which the wagons were painted to look like dazzle-camouflaged ships. Outside the military, interest in the subject grew—in part because it was a good fit with the Jazz Age—to the point of becoming inseparable from other zones of daily life, the arts in particular, as well as from subsequent social concerns.

For example, once the war had ended, among the most critical issues were the prohibition of alcohol (in the US) and the campaign for equal rights for women. In archival newspapers, one can find countless articles on the use of "camouflage" techniques (they were actually described as that) by rum-runners. At the same time, the edgy fearfulness of men toward advocates of women's rights prompted vehement articles on how women, since time immemorial, have used cosmetics, clothing and comparable sleights as camouflage in power workarounds with men.

A particularly detailed article on women's use of camouflage was published in the Washington Post in June 1919. Titled "Camouflage for Fat Figures and Faulty Faces," it was written and illustrated by American artist Alon Bement, who had been a major mentor for the painter Georgia O'Keeffe, and who had served in WWI as a ship camouflage designer. That same year, Bement published a

second article "Tricks by Which You Can Fool the Eye", which began with the following statement: "When you think of camouflage, you imagine it is something that belongs only to war. You probably have no idea that you can literally 'use it in your business,' that you can employ it in your houses, your yards and gardens, even in the clothes you wear."

There is a detailed discussion of the social assimilation of camouflage that took place after WWI in Regina Lee Blaszczyk's book, *The Color Revolution* (2012). Among other things, she shows how an American artist named H. Ledyard Towle, who had been an instructor during WWI for the Women's Reserve Camouflage Corps (the same group that had camouflaged the ship-shaped recruiting station), made a highly successful return to postwar civilian life. He repurposed his camouflage expertise toward improving industrial products (he developed durable and more colourful paints for kitchen appliances and cars), and thereafter had an affluent career as the first "corporate colourist" and as an "automobile stylist" at General Motors.

During the same era, parallel efforts were taking place in Australia, where prominent artists Sydney Ure Smith (who co-founded the Sydney Camouflage Group in 1938), Thea Proctor and George W. Lambert were commissioned by the Ford Motor Company to develop harmonious colour schemes for a new generation of Fords that appealed to more youthful consumers.

As for the military, their immediate interest in camouflage waned in the years between the World Wars. When WWII became a horrid reality, the technology of concealment had once again to get in step with advances in surveillance (and vice versa).

New Vision

Meanwhile, fine art had progressed toward abstraction on the one hand (remember Constructivism, the Bauhaus and Art Deco) and expressionism on the other. In WWII, artists were encouraged once again to volunteer as camouflage consultants, both military and civilian. Just as before, countless artists, designers and architects (on both sides of the conflict) contributed to wartime camouflage. György Kepes and László Moholy-Nagy taught civilian camouflage at the New Bauhaus in Chicago. Oskar Schlemmer painted camouflage for the Germans, while ironically being forbidden to make his own artwork, which had been banned as "degenerate." Arshile Gorky taught Gestalt-based camouflage in New York, until he was visited by the FBI, who were suspicious of how and why a non-citizen would have such knowledge and interest in a restricted military skill. Bill Blass and Ellsworth Kelly were recruited to be camoufleurs in WWII, but they served in a top secret unit (called the Ghost Army) that carried out what we might call "performance art." Their task was not so much to hide things, but to simulate things that didn't exist—using inventive multi-media tricks, they created the illusion of troop movements and other baffling non-events.

Throughout WWI, both art and camouflage had been based on unaided vision, more or less. By the end of WWII, the concept of "vision" had radically changed, mostly because of technologies that enabled humans to see things that were not visible before. Inevitably, military camouflage had to retrofit, while artists went on to progress on their own.

At the current time, art and artists are less traditional and more diverse than ever before. Once a conceptual sovereign state, art has precipitously become a spongy category. At the same time, military camouflage has become increasingly technological and non-visual (in the earlier sense). Today, the military is far more likely to consult tech-savvy scientists, gaming gurus, or computer-based technologists. As for scientific advances in camouflage—and, like it or not, the inevitable appropriation of those for military purposes—it appears that the current groundbreaking research is once again in the ballpark of technology and the biological sciences.

Current Developments

About fifteen years ago, a group of younger zoologists (most of them working in Europe) decided to set out to prove (or disprove) the camouflage hypotheses of Thayer and others, many of which (as it turns out) had never been closely examined. So they began to design rigorous experiments on such fundamental questions as: What is the function of zebras' stripes? Do creatures that blend with their background have a higher rate of survival? Does countershading really work? And so on. Their work in zoology is ongoing and expanding. But of particular value have been some surprising discoveries about the camouflage capabilities of cuttlefish, as studied by Roger Hanlon, and the wide array of experiments that have been reported in Martin Stevens and Sami Merilaita's *Animal Camouflage: Mechanisms and Function* (2009), and, more recently, in Stevens' *Cheats and Deceits: How Animals and Plants Exploit and Mislead* (2016).

There has also been a huge increase in books, films and magazine articles on the history, theory and cultural role of modern camouflage. Of particular note is Hardy Blechman's *Disruptive Pattern Material: An Encyclopedia of Camouflage* (2004), which includes a profusion of photographs of zoological, military, artistic and pop culture camouflage; in the boxed edition, there is even a second volume that is devoted entirely to the current camouflage-patterned military uniforms throughout the world.

Art historian Ann Elias has published books and articles on art and camouflage, notably Camouflage Australia: Art, Nature, Science and War (2011), in which, for example, she mentions the sometime reluctance of infantry men to make use of camouflage, because hiding was often considered to be cowardly or unmanly. Her research was a factor in the sponsorship by the Sydney College of the Arts (University of Sydney) in August 2013 of an international conference on camouflage, the results of which were published in Camouflage Cultures: Beyond the Art of Disappearance (2015), edited by Elias and her colleagues. Among the conference contributors was the Australian filmmaker Jonnie Morris, whose provocative documentary film, titled *Deception by Design* (2015), premiered on Australian television.

Of other recent camouflage books, among the most informative are Regina Lee Blaszczyk, *The Color Revolution* (2012); Hanna Rose Shell, *Hide and Seek: Camouflage, Photography and the Media of Reconnaissance* (2012); Laura Levin, *Performing Ground: Space, Camouflage, and the Art of Blending In* (2014); Cécile Coutin, *Tromper l'ennemi: L'invention du camouflage moderne en 1914-1918* (2015); Kevin M. Murphy, *Not Theories But Revelations: The Art and Science of Abbott H. Thayer* (2016); Rick Beyer and Elizabeth Sayles, *The Ghost Army of World War II: How One Top-Secret Unit Deceived the Enemy with Inflatable Tanks, Sound Effects, and Other Audacious Fakery* (2015); Jude Stewart, *Patternalia: An Unconventional History of Polka Dots, Stripes, Plaid, Camouflage and Other Graphic Patterns* (2015); Eviatar Zerubavel, *Hidden in Plain Sight: The Social Structure of Irrelevance* (2015); James Taylor, *Dazzle: Disguise and Disruption in War and Art* (2016); and Isla Forsyth, *Second World War British Military Camouflage* (2017).

Art and Camouflage Intersect

As confirmed by these and other sources, there are abundant experiments today in the nebulous categorical zone where art and camouflage intersect. The results can be astonishing, especially when the efforts are genuinely innovative and unprecedented. Understandably, as is the case in everything, some camouflage themes have become tiresome after being repeated for so many years by so many artists. Due in part to the non-stop exposure of internet images, there is the threat of the over-consumption of urban camouflage, sightseeing bloopers, and figure-and-wallpaper blending.

Similarly, with the arrival of the WWI Centenary in 2014, some revelers were threatened by an overdose of newly-painted dazzle ships. As often as not, the patterns had little or nothing to do with historic ship camouflage, with the memorable exception of Ciara Phillips' dazzling design "Every Woman" created for Edinburgh Art Festival 2016. Even work that revisits a familiar technique can be carried out inventively, as in the blending complexity in the photographs of Liu Bolin or in Cecilia Paredes' wallpaper paintings.

There is a refreshing oddity in the art museum camouflage of Harvey Opgenorth, in which he might study a painting in a major museum, design and build an outfit to blend in with the painting, then return to the same museum to have his picture taken while posing in front of the artwork. It was especially amusing when he camouflaged himself against an Ellsworth Kelly painting, because (as mentioned earlier) Kelly himself was a WWII camoufleur.

Back in the 1970s, David Bower made precisely crafted miniature rooms, added disruptive wallpaper, then camouflaged other components inside, including sheep in some of them. More recent are the animal camouflage artworks of Anne Lemanski. In the tradition of Abbott H. Thayer, she is as much a naturalist as an artist, and the tableau vivant poses of her sculpted animals are both poetic and persuasive.

7

Finally, it may not be undue to note that some of the finest camouflage art today occurs in works that do not claim to be camouflage-themed. One thinks of Joseph Podlesnik's on-site "drive by" camera shots in which (without the use of computers) he overlays "found" images and sandwiches components in the windows of retail stores, doors or reflective surfaces of cars. One can be equally awestruck by the photographic "set-ups" of Richard Koenig (like Thayer's countershaded ducks) in which he makes exacting use of the same reverse perspective tricks that were critical in the development of camouflaged ships in WWI.

"Camouflage is usually linked with military uniforms and inherently with violence and rigorousness. However, camouflage patterns are much more than a simple military feature. Its different forms can be observed and understood as an artistic product, both in terms of aesthetics and conceptuality. "

ALEXANDER MITCHELL @BACKWOODS GALLERY
A STUDY OF CAMOUFLAGE

A Study of Camouflage

In May 2015, Backwoods Gallery presented *A Study of Camouflage*, a new show within the *A Study of...* exhibition series.

A Study of Camouflage was the fourth exhibition in a row of the long-term project, which comprises annual shows that centre on different study subjects. Following the more than successful exhibitions *A Study of Hands*, *A Study of Eyes* and *A Study of Hair*, *A Study of Camouflage* focused on a completely different subject – camouflage.

With this exhibition series, we are creating a vivid archive of works by renowned artists from around the world whose works intersect on the same subject-matter. No matter the artistic style or technique used, a magnificent plurality of different approaches and representations of a single subject contextualises it, and places it in a dominant understanding of both the artists' and audience's views. Logically, this library becomes a diverse overview of different representations of a single subject, as seen and created by leading contemporary artists.

A Study of Camouflage brought together some of the leading contemporary artists whose art, in some way, touches the subject of camouflage. In collaboration with DPM-Studio (Disruptive Pattern Material), our concept sought to deconstruct the dominant perception of camouflage from its military driven narrative, and bring back the camouflage patterns to its natural roots. Camouflage is usually linked with military uniforms and inherently with violence and rigorousness. However, camouflage patterns are much more than a simple military feature. Its different forms can be observed and understood as an artistic product, both in terms of aesthetics and conceptuality. Aesthetically, camouflage can assume different shapes and forms, creating beautiful design and art products, while conceptually, it may be detached from its military connotation, and transformed to different purposes depending on the given context. Depending on the artistic approach, camouflage has enormous potentials for being a perfect medium for the countless interpretations of contemporary society. The use of camouflage in art may lead to more abstract forms, while on the other hand it can serve as the perfect material for figurative and conceptual approaches as well.

Each artist participating at *A Study of Camouflage* applied the concept of camouflage in different ways. The artists featured in the show were, in alphabetical order, Aaron De La Cruz, Acorn, Alexander Mitchell, Ashley Wood, Augustine Kofie, Beastman, Clemens Behr, Hardy Blechman, James Greenaway, Jaybo Monk, Jon Fox, Jun Inoue, Kano Hollamby, K-NARF, Madsaki, Mark Bode, Mark Drew, Masaho Anotani, MoneyLess, Nelio, O-Two, Petro, Rafael Sliks, Remi Rough, ROA, Senekt, SheOne, Shida, Shohei Takasaki, Shun Kawakami, Slicer, Stabs, Stephen Ives, TWOONE and Yusk Imai.

Alexander Mitchell @Backwoods Gallery

Alexander Mitchell is an Australian-born curator, photographer, filmmaker and artist. He has spent the last decade promoting and developing a community of artists in Australia and Japan. He naturally feels the need to organise things into groups with new meanings. As a curator he sorts artists and artwork, as an artist he sorts symbols.

Founded in 2010, Backwoods Gallery was originally a platform that supports the development and promotion of Australia's emerging street art scene. Located in in the Melbourne suburb of Collingwood, Australia, Backwoods offers a place where maverick artists can present their work on their own terms to a like-minded audience.

Acrylic and colour pencil on Arches 300gsm hot-pressed paper, 38 x 57cm

"BNP means 'Berlin night park', and 0.8 is my eyesight. With this eyesight at night after few drinks, everything I see can be camouflage."

Tsuri, Hiroyasu /TWOONE

Acrylic, coloured pencil and metal leaf on Arches 300gsm cold-pressed paper, 57 x 76cm

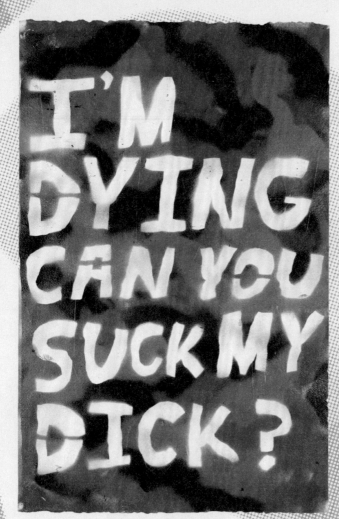

All: Aerosol and mixed media on Arches 300gsm cold-pressed paper, 57 x 76 cm

"Word War III, can't see sh#t. After nearly eight years in Tokyo, I barely notice the advertising — but it's always there, hidden in plain/plane sight."

Mark Drew

Travel brochure pages on Arches 300gsm hot-pressed paper, 38 x 57 cm

Travel brochure pages on Arches 300gsm hot-pressed paper, 57 x 76 cm

232

"Camo for me means a kind of contact with the nature and the texture of it. That concept has been part of my research for a long time."

Moneyless

Acrylic on Arches 300gsm hot-pressed paper, (Camo 2) 38 x 57 cm, (Camo 1) 57 x 76 cm

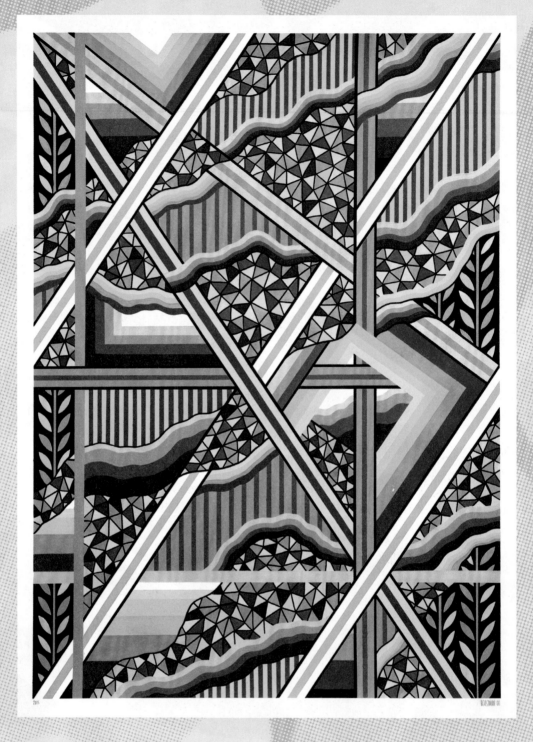

Acrylic on Arches 300gsm hot-pressed paper, 57 x 76 cm

"Camouflage is interesting by way of
it's used. It serves to hide as much as
it's used to attack."

Imai, Yusk

Fine liner on Arches 300gsm cold-pressed paper, 57 x 76 cm

"For me, camo is an interesting place where nature, art and war intersect."

Alexander Mitchell

Photo collage on Arches 300gsm hot-pressed paper, 57 x 76 cm

Acrylic and reflective aerosol on Arches 300gsm hot-pressed paper, 57 x 76 cm

"Fundamentally, camouflage is about being invisible, even in close-quarters. I was interested in the contrasts in its employment — in conflict and aggression, hunting and stalking — and in escape, self preservation, defence and cover. Real threats hidden in plain sight and vulnerabilities concealed against oppositions. Camo works best in static terms as motion undermines camo's concealing effect. I wanted to bring this movement to the piece: view it from a certain angle and the 3M reflective paint reveals certain details that were previously invisible. Take a flash photograph and see differences in the photograph that might not have been visible at the time."

O.Two

Sumi ink on Arches 300gsm cold-pressed paper, 57 x 76 cm

"The camouflage I designed is created based on the aggregation of one-stroke lines."

Inoue, Jun

Both: sumi ink on Arches 300gsm cold-pressed paper, 38 x 57 cm

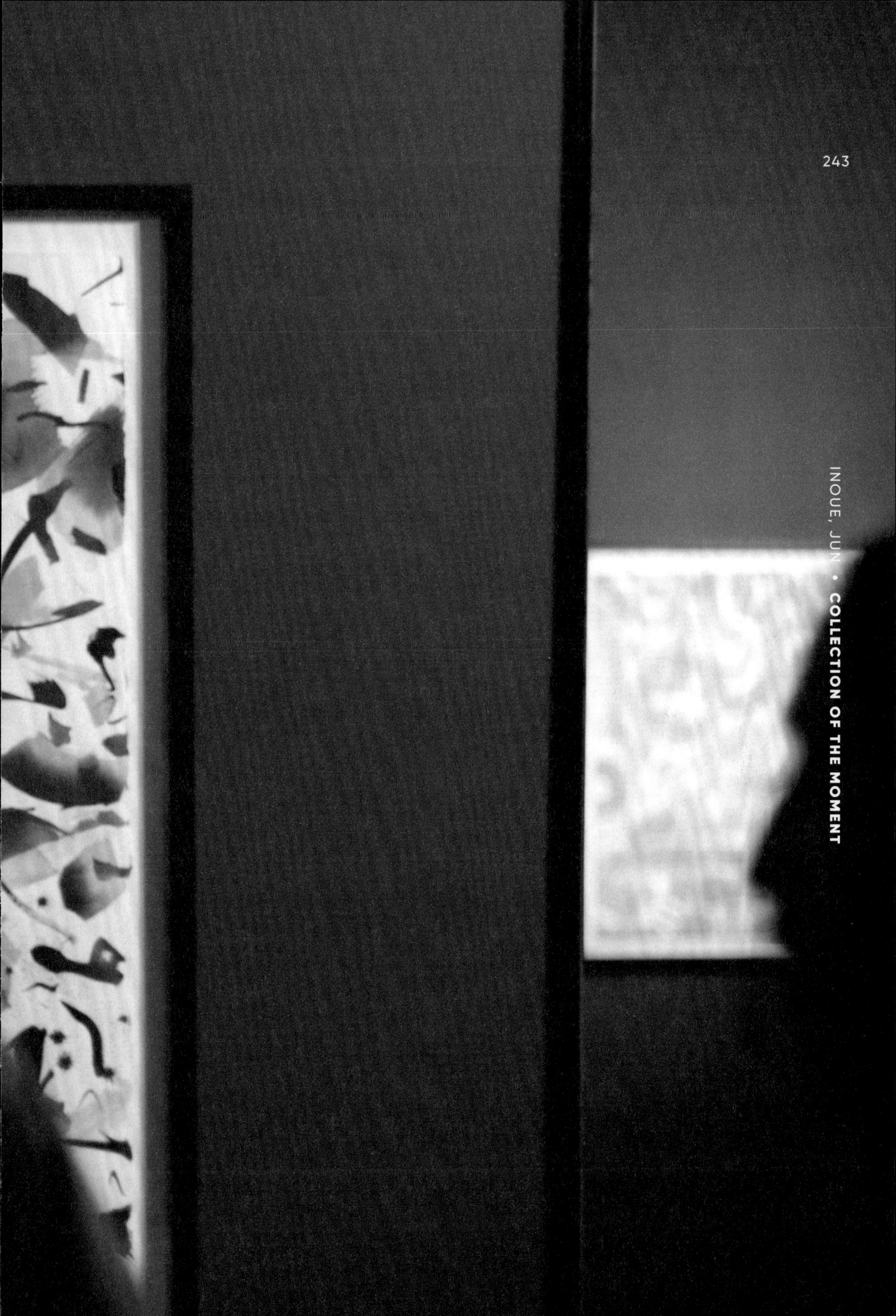

Ink and shellac on Arches 300gsm hot-pressed paper, 57 x 76 cm

"These studies are based on wildstyle tag writing techniques and, at the same time, inspired by aposematism or warning colouration and signals much like a poisonous redback spider would use to prevent attack and ward off potential harm from predators."

SLICER

SLICER • CAMOUFLAGE STUDY 1

> # "I am validating the abstraction of a military concept as contemporary art."

sheOne | blackAtelier

SHEONE | BLACKATELIER • JUPITER A / JUPITER C

Aerosol and acrylic on Arches 300gsm cold-pressed paper, (Jupiter A) 57 x 76 cm,
(Jupiter B & Jupiter C) 38 x 57 cm

Featured artists in
A Study of Camouflage

Alexander Mitchell
Beastman
Imai, Yusk
Inoue, Jun
Madsaki
Mark Drew
MoneyLess
O.Two
sheOne | blackAtelier
SLICER
Tsuri, Hiroyasu/TWOONE

Special credits

DPM-Studio

Biography

A-2-O Studio

Studio A-2-O was established by four graphic designers with a unique concept of graphic design and a strong desire to break with tradition. Their work appreciates strong conceptual ideas combining graphic design, photography and fine art. A-2-O devotes a lot of attention to search and create exceptional visual languages for each project. With a passion for music, art, theatre and cinematography, the team works with clients from across different industries.

Akatre

Founded by Valentin Abad, Julien Dhivert and Sébastien Riveron in 2007, Akatre is a creative studio based in Paris. The trio works and expresses themselves in graphic design, photography, typography, video, artistic installation and musical creation for institutions that works with art, culture, fashion, media and luxury.

Aktiva Design

Based in Barcelona, Aktiva provides talent, authenticity and quality. The studio is expert at design and creativity for premium products, and has over ten years of experience in developing multidisciplinary projects in the areas of branding, packaging, merchandising and POS advertising material for multinational leaders.

Apart

Apart is a Milan-based full-service communication agency founded by Micol Talso, Alessandra Mangini, Davide Mosconi and Andrea Mineo in 2011. Cooperation and talent development are central to Apart's philosophy, with associates all from leading international advertising companies. Apart aims to offer highly personalised and specialised service for customers, online and offline, and change people's mind with fascinating solutions where strategies, ideas and images meet.

Atelier Neşe Nogay

Atelier Neşe Nogay is an Istanbul-based creative studio founded in 2010. Specialising in book design, packaging, branding and art direction and with a passionate approach to projects, ranging from art and culture, fashion, food, beauty and print, the studio creates solutions that stand out in simple yet sophisticated visual aesthetics. The studio receives projects both locally and internationally, including New York, Paris, London and New Delhi.

Bielke&Yang

Bielke&Yang is an Oslo-based graphic design studio led by Christian Bielke and Martin Yang, specialising in visual identities, websites and printed matter. Small yet flexible and experienced, the team works closely with our clients throughout the design process. Bielke & Yang also flavours a diverse selection of clients and projects, from small startups to big companies with a long tradition.

Blanchard, Florence

Florence Blanchard is a French painter, muralist and screenprinter based in the UK. She began creating graffiti in the early 1990s under the alias, Ema, and spent ten years in New York where she completed her PhD at New York University in 2008. Her work is directly inspired by her training as a scientist and depicts abstracts molecular landscapes questioning the idea of visual perception.

Blok Design

Toronto-based design firm Blok expands the boundaries of design thinking with highly creative minds from around the world/ They work to take on initiatives that blend cultural awareness, and a love of art and humanity to advance society and business alike. Blok's work has been recognised internationally and exhibited in museums locally and in Tokyo.

BLOW

BLOW is a Hong Kong-based design studio founded by Ken Lo in 2010. Specialising in branding, identities, packaging, collaterals, environmental graphics, print, publications and website design, BLOW produces simple and inspiring designs. The studio believes that not only great ideas power design, but also the level of design craftsmanship. They aim at providing clients with single-minded, bold designs that communicate core ideas in a direct and effective approach.

Lang, Monika

Born in 1978 in Sombor, Serbia, Monika Lang received training in the department of illustration and book design in Belgrade. She worked as a freelance illustrator and graphic designer, chiefly on cultural projects, and is a member and co-founder of designer group Turbotomorrow, established in 2006.

Lee, Ken-tsai

Ken-tsai Lee is an assistant professor at National Taiwan University of Science and Technology (Taiwan TECH) and a local representative of The Type Directors Club and Art Directors Club New York. With a goal to connect Taiwan with the world, Lee introduces design exhibitions from overseas to Taiwan and put up design exhibitions in the region, reinforcing interactivity between Taiwan and the international scene.

Les Graphiquants

Founded in Paris in 2008, Les Graphiquants investigates and experiments with signs, and transform clients' stories into abstract, poetic, sensitive, black and white, sometimes colourful but always meaningful symbols with an inimitable dose of peculiarity. Their approach has always incited intelligent, brutal and delicate imagination combined with rigorous execution. Their expertise includes graphic design, typographies, identities, art direction, signage and websites.

Liefhebber, Nick

Nick Liefhebber is a Dutch graphic designer who produces campaigns, typefaces, illustrations and identities. With a belief in solving problems with creative ideas and design, he distills messages and creates unique stories. His work is also characterised by bold, fun and colourful illustrations. Drawn by patterns and rhythms, Liefhebber uses the associative powers of shapes and materials to communicate at an intuitive level, alongside images built as a collage of papercuts, ink drawings and computer generated imperfections.

Masi, Jérôme

Jérôme Masi is a French art director and illustrator. He has been working as a freelancer for twelve years.

Matsuyama, Shigeki

Born in 1973 and based in Kanagawa, Japan, Shigeki Matsuyama has been creating product illustrations and advertising freelance since 1998. Immediately after the 2011 Tohoku earthquake, Matsuyama held solo exhibition UNEASINESS in Tokyo, which inspired him to kick off his career as a conceptual artist. He is currently working with tableaux, objects and installation.

Mirror Mirror

Mirror Mirror is a branding and visual communication studio based in Antwerp. The multidisciplinary team creates and communicates brand identity for commercial, corporate and cultural clients imbued with clever concepts and striking graphic design.

Monge, Quentin

Quentin Monge runs Don't Try Studio.

Murmure

With offices in both Caen and Paris, MURMURE is a French creative communications agency known for creating strong visual identity. Led by art directors Julien Alirol and Paul Ressencourt, the agency helps client achieve their goals with unique and aesthetically pleasing creative solutions.

MWM Graphics

Matt W. Moore works to the credo of 'range is conducive to growth.' His background was in action board sports and the action art of graffiti, each with their core value lying in speed, do-it-yourself ethic, enthusiasm for new terrain, and the sheer fun of collaboration. Over the past decade, he has applied these principles to his bold, graphic aesthetic in media both analogue and digital. As the founder of MWM Graphics, Moore dubbed his digital abstract style 'Vectorfunk'. Many of his projects have been at the intersection of art and design, ranging from his own clothing line Glyph Cue, to projects such as the painted outdoor sculptures for Sretenka Design Week.

Nácher, Carmen

Based in Berlin, Germany, Spanish graphic designer Carmen Nácher specialises in photography, typography, illustration and packaging. Through colour, texture and composition, she renders idea in the most efficient and appropriate fashion. Her own projects often display a strong focus on her personal experiences and feelings.

Olek

Olek's art explores sexuality, feminist ideals and the evolution of communication through colours, conceptual exploration and meticulous detail. Olek consistently pushes the boundaries between fashion, crafts and public art, fluidly combining the sculptural and the fanciful. Drawing on the old-fashioned technique of crocheting, she takes the ephemeral medium of yarn to express everyday occurrences, inspirations and hopes. Her work is a metaphor for the complexity and interconnectedness of our body and psychological processes.

Pantone, Felipe

Argentinian-Spanish artist Felipe Pantone started doing graffiti at the age of twelve. With a fine art degree and a studio in Valencia, Spain, he travels the world ceaselessly with his art, where strong contrasts, vivid colours, effects, and mixed techniques combine to strike viewers. His work has been exhibited all over Europe, America, Australia, and Asia.

Perry, Leanna

Leanna Perry is a designer and artist based in Brooklyn, New York. Drenched in intricate hand-drawn patterns and bold graphics, Perry's work is infused with a lust for excess, urban exploring, street fashion, sweaty nightclubs, abandoned buildings, luxury textiles, deep house, and black metal. Her work has been appreciated by clients, including M·A·C Cosmetics, Forever 21, i-D Magazine, GAP, Urban Outfitters, Tidal Magazine, and 3M.

POOL

POOL is made of Léa Padovani (1981) and Sébastien Kieffer (1982). In their initial collaboration, the pair imagined the creation of their first objects that question their role as designers, the role of design itself and of objects in this world. Founded in 2010, POOL aims to explore relations between objects, architecture and images. Beyond the obvious presence of an object and its beauty and function, the duo searches for a multiplicity of meanings and highlights emotions and reference points.

Rehberger, Tobias

Born in 1966 in Esslingen, Germany, Tobias Rehberger attended Städelschule in Frankfurt, where he currently teaches. Through sculptures, industrial objects and handicrafts, he explores the wider sphere of structural design and architecture, thriving on chance connections and unexpected encounters. The process of perception, temporality, the sense of transience and the concept of transformation are all central to his art. His work that adorned Venice Biennale's café, done in collaboration with Artek, won him a Golden Lion award as best artist in 2009.

Rewell, Janine

Helsinki-based Janine Rewell has a weakness for geometry. Her style is characterised by pure vector lines that flirt with decorative shapes. Rewell's fantastical illustrations escape from paper onto human skin and into commercial campaigns and art galleries. Before freelancing in 2006, Rewell studied graphic design at the University of Art and Design Helsinki and the Rhode Island School of Design. Her designers have won awards at Red Dot Awards, Cannes Lions and ADC*E. Nike, Crate&Barrel, Vogue Eyewear, H&M, Toyota, and Finnair, have collaborated with Rewell.

RISOTTO

RISOTTO is a leading RISO specialist and stationery company in Scotland led by designer Gabriella Marcella. RISOTTO produces vibrant posters for wide-ranging clients. That includes leading art organisations, bands and brands. The house style is wonderfully playful, visible across its limited edition products, all bursting with vibrant colours and patterns.

Ronnie Alley Design

Graphic designer Ronnie Alley lives and works in Philadelphia. Branding, editorial design, and illustration take a fancy to him. Having graduated from Philadelphia University in 2016, Alley keeps himself busy as an in-house designer at JKRP Architects, while freelancing on the side. He can be mostly found conceptualising his next design project, hanging out with his cats, or eating too much at night.

Sagmeister & Walsh

Sagmeister & Walsh is an New York City-based design firm that creates brand identities, commercials, websites, apps, films, books and objects for clients, audiences and ourselves. We are a full service studio creating strategy and design across all platforms.

Yago, Naonori

Born in Shizuoka, Japan, in 1986, Naonori
Yago graduated from Musashino
Art University, Department of Visual
Communication Design in 2009, and joined
Hakuhodo as a designer the same year.
She is now an art director at SIX, inc. where
she has been working since 2013. She is a
recipient of Tokyo ADC award (2015), D&AD
Yellow Pencil, Cannes Lions Silver, ONE
SOHW Bronze, and New York ADC Bronze.

Page 078–079

ACKNOWLEDGEMENTS

We would like to thank all the designers and companies who have involved in the production of this book. This project would not have been accomplished without their significant contribution to the compilation of this book.
We would also like to express our gratitude to all the producers for their invaluable opinions and assistance throughout this entire project. The successful completion also owes a great deal to many professionals in the creative industry who have given us precious insights and comments. And to the many others whose names are not credited but have made specific input in this book, we thank you for your continuous support the whole time.

FUTURE EDITIONS

If you wish to participate in viction:ary's future projects and publications, please send your website or portfolio to submit@victionary.com